Playing with

"Storytelling is the great tree of civilization. Kevin Cordi has climbed all the branches of that tree. He is perfect for this book. I can't wait to hold it in my hands."

—**Jay O'Callahan**, storyteller, coach, author, and occasional NPR commentator

"Having participated in Kevin Cordi's workshops as both a parent and a teacher, I can attest to his unique capabilities as a storyteller and the limitless possibilities that he opens up through play. He moves seamlessly from directing a dozen students in an ever-evolving fairy tale to helping teachers write—and enact—their own stories. This book reminds us that creativity, expression and listening are more important now, in this age of standards and testing, than ever before."

—**Dr. Troy Hicks**, author of *Crafting Digital Writing: Composing Texts Across Media and Genres*

"Kevin Cordi is a master at playing with language through the power of storytelling. It is a great adventure to share his passion for using the imagination while crafting stories for all ages."

—**Mary Jo Huff**, author, storyteller & puppeteer

"In *Playing with Stories*, every fifth word Kevin Cordi said got me laughing in ways I wasn't expecting, and got me thinking about my story from a new perspective. While I was laughing my story was getting better and better. Kevin Cordi's great passion for story, his great passion for teaching and his great passion for laughter all come together in *Playing with Stories*."

—**Tony Toledo**, storyteller and former chair of the League for the Advancement of New England Storytelling

"The work of children is play! Kevin Cordi has incorporated this concept into his professional work to a fantastic degree. He integrates this tool of Story/Play into a seamless flow that teaches even adults to loosen up a bit when using the ancient art of storytelling in the 21st century."

—**Bobby Norfolk**, Emmy Award-winning storyteller

"Kevin Cordi is the real deal. For decades, he's worked and played with tellers young and old, challenging them and himself to mess with story as potters mess with clay. Let yourself play with Cordi's imaginative prompting. Kevin Cordi knows the power of imagination, having coached the wonderfully messy work of shaping story with others for decades. If you let it, this book will lure you to new places as teacher and artist."

—**Marni Gillard**, author storyteller, story teacher

"Kevin Cordi, a master in the field of story development, is famous for his work in improving storytelling in education and for encouraging youth troupes. I travelled halfway across the globe to hear his stories and seek his wisdom, all of which exceeded expectation."

—**Terrie Howey**, England

"Kevin offered his Permission to Play workshop for our guild this past spring. We played and played and played, and afterwards, we were dumbfounded at how much work we'd gotten done!"

—**Mary Grace Ketner**, San Antonio Storytellers' Association

"Kevin Cordi lives in the world of story and invites us all—teachers, students, writers—to enter that world with him. Through play, imagination, and his story box project, he leads us to the traditional world of story … and beyond to the world of story we create. This book will help educators at many levels find his power to transfix, transport and transform us through story."

—**Robin Holland**, author of *Deeper Writing*

"Kevin Cordi is one of the pioneers of storytelling in education. He's one of our great encouragers, always inviting new voices into the circle of storytellers."

—**Dan Yashinsky,** Canadian storyteller and author of *And Then They Heard Footsteps*

Playing with Stories

**Story-crafting for storytellers, writers, teachers
and other imaginative thinkers**

Kevin D. Cordi, Ph.D.

Parkhurst Brothers Publishers

MARION, MICHIGAN

www.parkhurstbrothers.com

Parkhurst Brothers books are distributed to the trade through the Chicago Distribution Center, and may be ordered through Ingram Book Company, Baker & Taylor, Follett Library Resources and other book industry wholesalers. To order from Chicago Distribution Center, phone 1-800-621-2736 or fax 800-621-8476. Copies of this and other Parkhurst Brothers Inc., Publishers titles are available to organizations and corporations for purchase in quantity by contacting Special Sales Department at our home office location, listed on our web site. Manuscript submission guidelines for this publishing company are available on our web site.

Printed in the United States of America
First Edition, 2014
2014 2015 2016   10 9 8 7 6 5 4 3 2 1

Library of Congress Cataloging-in-Publication Data

Cordi, Kevin.
 Playing with stories : story-crafting for storytellers, writers, teachers and other imaginative thinkers / Kevin D. Cordi. —First Edition.
     pages cm
 Summary: "It has not been easy to value play. Mainstream culture urges us to rush and finish what we are working on to quickly advance to the next task at hand. Too often we must punch our time clock forward without much consideration. As the minutes and hours move, we indirectly communicate both to ourselves and the world no time remains to play; we must work. Despite that the world around me does not value play, in my creative life, play is necessary. In fact, I have discovered it is the real work I do as an artist and teacher. As a storyteller, writer, teacher, and imaginative thinker, it is play that has produced the most desired results in my life, in my work, and especially, in my creativity. It is in play that we experience who we are and we begin to extend our choices. Play is not consciously prepared; discovery that happens in the moment. It invites reflection. In fact, Plato once shared, "You can discover more about a person in an hour of play than in a year of conversation."   In this book, you will discover new ways to work with your story craft and find new story direction using play. Indeed, play is a meaningful way to create and learn. In both childhood and adult play, the imagination plays a central role in the meaning making process. Although there are many types of play: school-based, recess, sports, this work is rooted in play inviting the writer, storyteller, or imaginative thinker to make choices as they work to create meaning in their work. I will share how collaborative play can increase your choices when making a story. You will find not only exercises to build your story-making and telling skills, but pedagogy of practice to use when called to create story. "—Provided by publisher.

 Summary: "An educator's manual for teachers, leaders and students of oral storytelling arts developed by a Ph.D. professor who has worked extensively with all ages K-16"— Provided by publisher.
 ISBN 978-1-62491-049-4 (hardback) -- ISBN 978-1-62491-037-1 (trade paperback) -- ISBN 978-1-62491-038-8 (e-book)
 1. Storytelling--Study and teaching. I. Title.
 LB1042.C495 2014
 372.67'7--dc23
                                  2014016380
This book is printed on archival-quality paper that meets requirements of the American National Standard for Information Sciences, Permanence of Paper, Printed Library Materials, ANSI Z39.48-1984.

While the author has made every attempt to provide accurate Internet addresses at the time of publication, neither the publisher nor the author assumes any responsibility for errors or changes that occur after publication. Further, the publisher does not have any control over and does not assume any responsibility for author or third party websites or their content

Cover photo by: Matthew Heller
Cover design by: Rebecca Bobb
Page design by: Rebecca Bobb and Linda D. Parkhurst PhD
Acquired for Parkhurst Brothers Publishers by   Ted Parkhurst
Edited by: Elaine Muray

This book could not be written without the support of my wife,

Barbara Allen.

She reminds me that play is the greatest work that we can do.
Most of all, she constantly reminds me that
play is best achieved together.

Acknowledgements

Mr. and Mrs. Lyle G. Cordi—without you, none of my stories would be told. Dad and Mom, you are my true teachers!

Rives Collins of Northwestern University—you first showed me the value of play and drama as it relates to story. This is a lesson I continue to explore. Your work speaks volumes.

Brian Edmiston of Ohio State University—you demonstrate the fusion between learning and play. The time I spent with you will affect all I do.

Amy Shuman of Ohio State University—your confidence in my work moves me to create better work. Your sage counsel is deeply appreciated and respected.

My team at the Columbus Area Writing Project—a playground to learn not only to be writers, but work as a community. David Bloome, Robin Holland, George Newell, and Melissa Wilson—you bring energy and focus to my work.

I would like to acknowledge the work of Ted Parkhurst and Parkhurst Brothers Publishers. Ted, you bring not only this book to educators and imaginative thinkers, but countless others. You are one of the main reasons that storytelling and storytellers have a voice.

To contributors Simon Brooks, Flavia Everman, and Kris Hillenburg—I am deeply indebted to you.

Thank you to Elaine for your second eye on this work. Your comments only made it clearer.

It is a great joy to me to be alongside the remarkable adults and students I have coached—mediated—and learned from in my over twenty-seven years of working with story.

Each new day brings promise because of these people and so many others I have had the pleasure of working with in my journey of discovery. Thank you for informing the work of play and story.

Contents

Chapter 1
My World of Play—Giving Permission to Play

Why We Should Use Play

    I was raised on my West Virginian parents' Appalachia stories. My five brothers and sisters and I would gather on our dilapidated old couch to listen as my father and mother would regale us with stories. I would sit spellbound in my old chair listening to Grandpa tell how he killed an old black snake hiding out behind the barn or laugh out loud as my mother recalled the time my sister took a giant bite out of a solid hard block of chewing tobacco, thinking it was candy. Each night was entertaining and educational. We traveled to the days of yesterday and today. We really listened to the stories. As much I savored this experience, we didn't wrestle with making our own stories. We didn't create them together, but we listened deeply to what was said. This has helped me realize the value of deep listening to mediate and orchestrate play for and with others. Before play begins, a storyteller or writer must know how to listen for the story and later listen to where play would work to help accentuate it. In this book, I share methods to strengthen deep listening skills to build and focus the craft of storytelling.

    It has not been easy to value play. Mainstream culture urges us to rush and finish what we are working on to quickly advance to the next task at hand. Too often we must punch our time clock forward without much consideration. As the minutes and hours move, we indirectly communicate both to ourselves and the world that no time remains to play. We must work. For in work, many tasks get done. Parents rush to prepare young kids to "grow up" and act their age. Recess is eliminated as kids mature. Time is spent preparing young adults for college or to be a democratic participant in the country and hopefully, the world. More time is dedicated to reducing playtime in favor of the work involved to be successful.

Teachers train students to seek answers, but not how to answer questions naturally developed through play. We expect people to simply know how to relate to others because they have been taught or we modeled it. We do not use role or playful techniques to explore what would happen if somebody became angry or confused. Instead, by sheer osmosis we expect him or her to know what to do or how to behave in any situation. Some of us develop this ability. But if it does not happen, we don't engage in any rehearsal of the situation. We let things happen and rarely have time to reflect, let alone replay the action. Play provides a chance to review and even change our actions, but it is rarely used.

In many occupations even the thought of pausing our work to play with the ideas of yesterday before beginning the work of today would only invite laughter. We cannot ask for more time of our English teachers for an essay assignment because we are playing with the ideas. The clock ticks on and we feel forced to answer. Regardless, spending time playing with our ideas will help bring fruitful results. So we press forward. With play, time is dedicated to reconsider and redesign a work decision. Still the modus operandi is to move on without play.

We evaluate others based on the number of tasks they complete. Assignments are assigned. Work consists of tasks. In my creative life play is necessary, even though the world around me does not value play. In fact, I have discovered that play is the real work I do as an artist and teacher. As a storyteller, writer, teacher, and imaginative thinker, it is play that has produced the most desired results in my life, in my work, and especially in my creativity. Through play we experience who we are and begin to extend our choices. Play is not consciously prepared. It is discovered in the moment. It invites reflection. In fact, philosopher Plato once shared, "You can discover more about a person in an hour of play than in a year of conversation."

Play as my Guide
Play has been my guide for years, shaping my work and creating my

identity as a storyteller, writer, and teacher. Through play, I transform into an imaginative thinker.

The Importance of Play and Writing

In high school, I read from the traditional "dead white writers" cannon and was required to memorize the details of their major works. I also remember when I asked what it meant to be a writer the teacher replied, "You will never make the mark of these writers, but the best preparation is to read as much as possible." He told me not to try writing, but rather to read as much as I could. I did read, but I read so slowly. With each book, I felt more distance from becoming a writer myself.

Over the years, I did not value my skills. Sometimes, even now, I still fight to be encouraged by my writing. It is easy to think I can't be a writer, but now I draw on the idea that writers should invite play with ideas in order to complete them. The first draft is not the last. The revision and reflection that occurs in play will improve the outcome of the work.

It is hard at times, to envision yourself as a writer. When this happens to me, I am reminded of the time I took a class in creative nonfiction by the science fiction author Geoffrey Landis. We traded our writing every week and without signing our names, shared feedback. I will never forget the stark words on my paper: "You call yourself a teacher of writing; I would never take your class." I felt the sting of those words. There was no play in these comments.

When someone provides comments like this, there is no room for change. It is simply a declaration of someone who needs to say something; it has little to do with helping a person with his or her craft. It was important for this person to tell me—unsigned—that I did not meet her standards. When I confided this to Landis, I will never forget his response, "You know, it was in your mistakes that your writing came alive for me." He praised the detail in my story about a homeless man called "The Gutter Fish." He liked the mistakes in language choices because it enhanced the dialogue of the man. He said that awkward sentence construction was easy to fix—what I did have was a solid idea, and from this idea, finer details. He encouraged me to play with these ideas even if my first attempts were mistakes. He invited me to take risks. I know this contributed to the value I place on play. As I began to see myself as a playful writer, I ignored those people who felt they had to declare comments about my writing, and instead work with others who helped me by providing permission for me to explore my writing and my choices. Listening to these advisors helped me believe I had something to say and that I would need to use play to refine the words.

Before, I believed reading the "widely read bookshelves" of a bookstore would make me a good writer. I worked to make this happen, but looking back, I spent more time knowing I was not a certain type of writer, so I didn't try. Like so many, I was fearful to show my writing to someone until it was ready, which did not occur often. The English teacher said I should read as much as I could to become a writer. As a writer, I do more than read. As a writer, I observe, note, write, reflect, remember—and most of all, play. Reading is valuable but so is examining what we write. Trying it out and recasting in other ways can move the direction of the story.

For the last seven years, I have served as a co-director for the Columbus Area Writing Project at Ohio State University. Every summer, we head off to Kenyon College for a writing retreat with K-college teachers. Before the retreat we provide interviews to get to know the teachers and gauge why they elected to be involved in the writing institute. The expectation is that we involve those who are serious writers or at least serious about writing. This is not always the case. We often invite teachers who simply want to know more about writing and how they can provide better ways for their students to write. What we tell them—but they also soon discover and experience—is that we not only learn about writing, but we work together as writers. We provide time to play with the writing, so as to build a community of support. We partner with them as they write, rewrite, reflect, and revisit their own work.

When people are provided with this time, they are amazed at what happens. Too often the third grade teacher is awed from the response when she reads a poem about her old home and the impact it has on everyone that listens. A high school teacher is so taken by the story written the day before and immediately wants to share it with the larger writing group. We engage in quick writes and students experiment with styles and forms of their work. We create a community where voices are honored in the writing—and telling— process. They are invited to revisit and reposition their first drafts as we spend the next two weeks playing with our words.

Under the direction of my colleagues, David Bloome, Robin Holland,

George Newell, and Melissa Wilson, we form writing groups to bounce around our ideas and play with our choices. I have spent countless hours devouring rough drafts or working with Robin Holland, another co-director, and author of *Deeper Writing* (2013), as she demonstrated new ways to create writing that has a greater impact.

It is here I also learned what happens when someone supports you, without their own agenda, as you explore writing choices. Too often we don't learn from and with each other. This is a place where we orient our direction. This is important for anyone involved in the craft of writing and telling. Writers, tellers, and other imaginative thinkers need to have room to write, speak, and basically create without judgment. If a person is negatively evaluated on their work, especially in the early stages, the creativity can stop. Story-crafters need to be surrounded by caring communities seeking partners that honestly support their choices.

At the Columbus Area Writing Project, I found it to be a place where I realized how important it is to develop a playful environment when a person wants to be creative. After all, this is our goal if we write for publication, but does it develop us as creative artists? Too often, people gather for the sole purpose of getting into print, but is this the only reason for which we create? Do we always have to seek out publication to be valued? When we strip the ego out of the environment and work from the position that there is something in all of us that is creative, we begin to build creative work. Only in this environment can our words dance.

Play in Many Forms—Ways to Make the Words Dance

As artist Pablo Picasso once said, "Painting is another way of keeping a diary." Picasso played with images, and so does the imaginative thinker when it comes to writing or telling stories. With language, we need to let the words dance. Words need to have freedom to be released from print. They need to soar, sprint and especially, dance. Now, as I write, there are times when I need to dance with the words. I feel the wonder that happens when I share my ideas with another person. I let the words rest while I tell the story of what I want to create. In play, I become a better writer because I don't merely write the words, I invite the words to live within other forms and dance before they meet the page.

In play, I can draw what I say. I can use drama to move the words and make better sense because of the choices I make. In play, I can invite others to listen and recall my choices. In play, not only do the words dance, but I also dance. I can use many forms to help me see my story unfold.

In this book, many exercises will be shared that have supported my *word dancing* over the years. I will share pedagogy of practice using play. Use them; let them change as you work with them. Word dancing happens when creating ideas and exploring choices. You, in a sense, move the words to the rhythm of your choices. Instead of immediately penning an idea, I will draw on many methods to see the words unfold. The dance is required to explore choices.

Deep Listening:

Before the words can dance, we must develop deep listening skills. When there is deep listening everything goes away except the story and the connection between teller and listener. Remember those times when a teacher or a family member began talking and everything disappeared? You weighed in on each word. This can be established at a good poetry reading, story slam, or simply a telling of the day. However, as a teller, there are ways to establish deep listening invitations. This book shares ways to improve the telling skills to invite this type of listening. However, this is only one side of deep listening. There is also the type of coach or listener who invites personal and connected responses. This is the beginning point of reflection when the coach or another teller lets go of what is on his or her mind to help focus on the teller's story development. This can occur in quiet listening circles, but it can also be done with a group of tellers. Deep listening with a coach can help the teller find new directions.

I learned and developed this from listening to the best storytelling coaches in the country. I worked personally with dynamic storytelling coaches such as Doug Lipman, Marni Gillard, Chuck Larkin and countless others. Each coach had his or her own style—some vastly different than others—but all of them shared acute listening skills. The best coaches first listened to your needs and from what was said, used these ideas to engineer the coaching. I learned from these collections of coaches plus my own ways of deep listening to develop "Permission 2 Play"—www.permission2play.com. This employs not only deep listening, but also a way to *mediate*, my term for coaching stories as works in progress. It is a practice that employs process drama and the story-making processes that I have studied and taught in my over twenty-eight years of working with story. It draws heavily upon my doctoral work at Ohio State University employing dramatic methods and inquiry in the story-making processes. What is valued most in this work is the simple but powerful understanding that the coach, whom I call the *mediator*, works to help the teller. The mediator is not there to show a fancy trick or clever word use; instead he or she is there to serve the teller. The mediator honors the teller's needs and abilities throughout the process. The models and exercises in this text serve the teller to improve his or her story craft.

Use of Play in the Classroom

There should be more play in the classroom. Unfortunately, as a high school teacher for fourteen years, I was more schooled in the discipline of creating final products instead of what it meant to play with making the products work. In other words, we evaluate the end result, but what we really should consider perhaps even more, is the process of creation. The design or the craft of how something is achieved strengthens the way students will produce later. It also develops a deliberate mindset that the classroom is a place to practice as much as to produce work. What was accentuated was the performance. What was missing were the playful processes that were used not only to create performance, but also to learn. Our education system, driven by standards and mandates, is more concerned with outcomes than development. This was most felt in the nationwide and statewide efforts to standardize learning. I watched the creative vein drain from some of my colleagues as we pushed out creative methods for our students to learn.

Standardization of learning was the state and federal mandate. Students were feeling this pressure too. In fact, it was actually students who showed me the need and desire for play, especially when it came to working with story in the schools. Over the years, I have discovered that students who use play to exceed the state standards reconsider and rethink and even redo work so that is understood. Using play, learning becomes an active process of engagement. Research supports the fact that the more active students are in the learning process, the more reflective they become.

As a storyteller and storytelling teacher, stories were the way that I taught. Students organically understood the natural flow of narrative. They know story as the way in which they learn. From when they were little, they were immersed in a narrative environment. Why not use it for teaching? It was and is the most effective method to grab a student's attention, but also to invite investment in the material.

It was an early morning class and I was teaching at East Bakersfield High School in California when a young freshman, Jennifer Wooley, approached me and said, "Mr.Cordi, you tell stories in every class I have had with you." As I explained to her how much value stories have, she interrupted, "I want to do more with stories than tell them in class. Could we have a storytelling club after school?" She detected my confusion on how to start, but Jennifer said, "Don't worry Mr. Cordi, I have it handled."

One week later, she had our first meeting planned—telling ghost stories for thirty minutes in a dark, dank basement. Four and half hours later—of laughing and simply having fun telling and retelling stories—the next meetings were planned. From then on the students and I met on a weekly basis. We became a storytelling club: Voices of Illusion.

What about Listening to Students?

For eleven years, I coached students for five to twenty hours a week after school. Later, when I taught storytelling classes during school, there was no set curriculum. I built our objectives based on what I knew about storytelling and what I had discovered after years of attending storytelling conferences, festivals, and events. At first, I was content to have the students prepare a story and then tell it. However, the students began to ask about adding rap lyrics, music and even dance. They did not have my prior experience with regard to how a story must be told. Instead, they wanted to use and include other arts to build a story. In my past, I had been taught that storytelling could not include dance or puppets.

I remember when the talented group Eth-Noh-Tec, Robert Kikuchi-Yngojo and Nancy Wang entered the national storytelling world. They combined Asian style dance into their story work. I remember some of my colleagues questioned if this was storytelling, while others accepted it. It did not look like what storytelling looked like then. Over time, this talented group showed the value of being different. Although they used old art forms, including story and dance, they made it look new as they integrated it with story. They helped break new ground in storytelling. Today the rules are shifting. More and more fields are opening to the possibilities of storytelling. Again, it does not look the same, but is new. My students in my storytelling clubs and troupes over the years have taught me to value the arts alone and in connection with story. In our work they did not worry about the unspoken rules. They only wanted to play with making a story by fusing crafts from other disciplines.

We told stories in small groups, developed listening partners, and created ways to word dance with ideas. In other words, I created more playful choices in the developing phase of story. Over time, I learned there are numerous ways to create a story and we began to play with these choices. In our weekly meeting, students would share rap, use a flute to echo the sounds of a bird in a Cherokee myth, include drums, symbols, puppets, and even develop stories in groups of twenty-five or more.

My students work together. Although at the time adult storytellers would only tell alone—and many still tell only solo—I can still remember Andrew and Steven creating laugh riot routines when telling "No News" adapted by the Folktellers and expanding each line in a rapid rhythm reminiscent of "Who's on first?" Groups of four, and later up to even twenty-five students began to create a story from a spark. They built story from improvised ideas and directions. In creating a full three-hour program on flight, we had over twenty-four students tell the story from the Wright brothers to future flights to Mars. Students added dance, popular news headlines, and ensemble work that was not common in storytelling circles.

As we played, the students' listening grew. This was evidenced by how their language changed dramatically as we engaged in playful exercises. Student Chris told a story about a polar bear and instead of hearing, "It was good or he liked the sound of the bear," other students offered to mirror the voices of other bears for him. Another student stood as tall as he could so that Chris could imagine the bear even more. My students were playing inside the story world. For Chris, instead of listening to him tell the story, they worked with him to make the story more real and alive. A conversation began. When Chris next told his story, he included some of these ideas. The story still stays with me because of its authenticity.

Another student, Jessica, a German exchange student, worked with the urban legend that outlined an unknown caller who asks, "Have you checked the children?" Later the story reveals that the call comes from inside the house. When we played with the story, a symphony of voices joined in her urban legend thundering even more the call of "Have you checked the children?" My teenagers turned into a dozen children running away. Jessica sounded stronger because of the voices behind her. As an ensemble, we worked to improve the story. We grew from there.

We created full length CDs through the process of play. We needed to spend time not only telling stories, but creating together. We had to play in order to truly see the storytelling experience come alive. My students began to play with their own versions of stories, recorded professional audio and videotapes, and toured throughout the state of California and beyond. It was when we played with our ideas as a group and learned from the direction of our play that my student youth storytelling clubs and troupes became models for youth storytelling.

Our reputation grew. I became and served, according to the National Storytelling Network, as "the first full-time high school storytelling teacher in the country." In all my classes, I began to value not only the narrative I was telling, but also the narratives I created with and for my students. Our storytelling class became a model for others to follow for those using narrative structure in and out of the classroom. We always included play to shape our understanding of story. Realizing that storytelling is more than telling—it is about the storytelling experience—what makes up that experience is what a high school student Allison called "focused freedom" (Adler, 2009, 1) that occurs in the story-making process. This is where one allows many choices to be explored so he or she has freedom to explore choices with support to help focus the ideas. This is focused freedom to create with direction.

A storytelling experience is an experience that allows students to explore choices in the shaping and telling of a story. Students, instead of being directed on the right line or next cue, are free to explore. But they have a coach, guide or what I like to call a *story mediator* to help the shape of the work. This is what I have become. Vygotsky stated that when two or more students are involved in problem-based play, students would become a "head taller in their learning" (1978,102). This is accentuated when someone helps scaffold the learning. This scaffolding develops when storytellers study the craft of story-making. However, in order to enhance the craft, one must do more than learn a story from a printed page and then tell it later for an audience.

The Value of the Story-Making Process

In my classroom, instead of producing a show of creativity, we examined the craft and design involved in making someone creative. When I was teaching *The Odyssey*, instead of having the students create a traditional book report, I gave them focused freedom to choose how they would represent this. I did this by providing parameters for what they made. For example, they needed to retell the story, but I gave them freedom on how they represented it. I vividly remember my students making a film using Ninja Turtle action figures in the bathtub and watching Homer's tale unfold in the bathtub water current. The storm was created with a push in the water so we could see the perils of the journey. I provided the freedom for them to explore the work their way. They had the freedom to play and still learned the ideas.

When I was teaching Chaucer's *Canterbury Tales,* we created our own tales and composed characters like Chaucer, but ours wore cheerleading and band uniforms. We transformed our class into a modern Mead Hall. We collected ghost stories in our neighborhood of Hanford, California and told them around a campfire. It is from teaching storytelling that I realized story-making was just as important as storytelling. When I had to create daily storytelling lessons, I learned to explore and play with the way stories were used not only in performance, but for learning as well.

Unfortunately, at a time when we need to value story-making, we are turning again to standardization. As a university professor in the education division at Ohio Dominican University for the past seven years, I again see the need to introduce standards for learning instead of teaching pre-service teachers the value of flexible planning with play. As I travel around the country, teachers and administrators decry that they have no time for play when they have to build curriculum to meet local, state, and national mandates. Some educators and administrators have forgotten that working to find an answer is not as fruitful as working to discover how and why we need to be more critical in our learning. They have forgotten the value of play. This book serves as powerful reminder on how play can be reinstituted in the classroom.

If you are teacher, you should read this book to rekindle the playful work in your classroom. The first step is to realize that you too, are an imaginative thinker.

Imaginative Thinking

How often in our classrooms, workplaces, and even family life are we asked to be imaginative? It is sometimes hard to remember the last time we were asked to create something new from playing with choices. What would you do if your boss, a teacher, or even your father said, instead of filling out that report, writing that research paper or mowing the grass, "Let me give you the day to come up with a new idea for what you are doing. How about you taking some time to imagine your choices?" I know many of you are saying: "I have no time to use my imagination, I have work to do." In this book, I argue that using your imagination is some of the most powerful work you will do, especially when it comes to creating stories. Instead of depending on the pen or computer, I want to demonstrate and share how dancing with your ideas will help you find not one choice, but many, to direct your stories.

With some basic guiding principles, a pedagogy of practice will be established that allows you to not only imagine as you solely create, but also to have the skills to help others deeply listen to your story, and allow you to become what I call a story mediator that helps you play with the story.

Drawing on educational socio-constructivist Lev Vygotsky (1978) who believes in problem-based play, this pedagogy will equip others to wrestle with the dramatic tensions (Heathcote, 1984) that are inherent in story. You will also be able to imagine perspectives and possible tensions that will strengthen the work of your story. Imagination drives the story.

If we didn't make time for writing and telling stories, I would caution with what poet Sylvia Plath states, "What I fear most, I think, is the death of the imagination" (2000, 204). How can we create as writers, storytellers, and creative artists, if we don't allocate time for play? After all, it is the imagination that allows us to create.

> Imagination has brought mankind through the Dark Ages to its present state of civilization. Imagination led Columbus to discover America. Imagination led Franklin to discover electricity. Imagination has given us the steam engine, the

telephone, the talking-machine and the automobile; for these things had to be dreamed of before they became realities. So I believe that dreams - daydreams, you know, with your eyes wide open and your brain-machinery whizzing - are likely to lead to the betterment of the world. The imaginative child will become the imaginative man or woman most apt to create, to invent, and therefore to foster civilization. (Baum, *The Lost Princess of Oz*, 1990, 615)

How Does One Become an Imaginative Thinker?

In order to imagine, we must first become imaginative thinkers, dedicating just as much time if not more to the *how* and *why* created not just the *what*. A writer that I recently met said to me, "I never share my writing out loud. If I say it out loud, I let it go and it is no longer mine. I don't want to let it go." This freezes the ideas and limits imaginative thinking. As my storytelling friend and colleague Rafe Martin once said, "Stories are trapped in books. It is the storyteller who sets them free". When developing stories, let them dance, fly, and roam in unknown places because it is in the discovery and suspense that all stories must build. All stories hinge on suspense, something that makes the reader or listener curious to know more. By playing with tension, the suspense can be elevated or decreased. Canadian storyteller Dan Yashinsky speaks to the allure and magical power when he is telling his child a soft story to put him to sleep and just as he thinks he is resting, he bolts upright and declares, "And then they suddenly heard footsteps." We want those footsteps to be heard in our story but we don't provide enough spaces for suspense to happen. We need to express our work in so many ways so that even in the development we build anticipation, suspense and release.

Play creates spaces to release stories. There are endless possibilities to explore when writing and telling a story. Why be limited to saying it out loud or penning it to paper? I talked with middle school Newberry award-winning author Richard Peck and asked him about his process. He stated he always talks out his stories before he writes them down. He says that as he types, he imagines the scene. He takes time to see and hear his words before they are in print. In this book, we value talking out loud to explore shaping stories. We do more than imagine. We share exercises and proven skillful methods to move the story to experience it as though it is occurring now. We will use our imagination to skillfully see the world of the story unfold and use play to make it real.

Value the Process of Play

Writers and storytellers are more concerned how a finished story sounds and less with the methods used to create it. Once a story is written, only then do we release it to an audience. It is sent to a prospective publisher or told to a new listening audience. As a writer and teller, I first would spend endless hours over a computer or a piece of paper as I drafted and redrafted different versions of my story. I would slave over the right word, the best turn of a phrase or plot line that I could create and write—or type—on my paper. I prided myself on my method of learning a story. I had a pattern down and I thought it suited me. The question is, did this help me to become more of an imaginative thinker?

Stepping Inside the World of the Story

My organized standard pattern of writing or telling a story was shaken when I enrolled in a story and drama class at Northwestern University where professor/storyteller Rives Collins was teaching. Without a formal announcement, we were immersed in story in a class designed around play. He immediately took on the role of a man looking for people to travel west with him. He dramatically announced we would earn money so we could settle the West. Without writing a single word or even having a discussion about plot or character, we became travelers trying to survive in the West. He became our eyes as he mediated us against talking with or combating against the Natives and demonstrating our choices of what we might choose when our wagon lost a wheel. With his dramatic directing, he helped us craft our story as to how we could survive eating a poison root, and later how we could start settling in this unknown land.

Rives mediated our story-based world. However, we could choose what we did in this world. We were free to suggest and even enact our choices. Together we decided what happens when one of our travelers ate poison or needed extra attention because they were injured in the journey. We were no longer observers in the drama. Everyone was involved playing, making our story world come alive. We used inquiry and imaginative design to reshape, rethink, and reactivate this world to be present within the room. In fact, the room changed into that of the Old West and instead of being students, we were surviving the trials and tribulations that came from walking the trail.

Up until this time, I viewed storytelling as a something that occurred as people sat in a circle. But this was not the storytelling that occurred. This was a time when the story was made by the choice of an entire group. Introducing dramatic tension, we examined more choices in creating the story. The story was not written or memorized; it emerged out of our focused play. With the help of a mediator, the story changed, shifted, and unfolded through choices made by the entire group. This was a new way for me to see how story-making could be used to develop stories with my students.

Carl Sagan reminds us, "Imagination will often carry us to worlds that never were, but without it we go nowhere" (Cosmos, 1980). I encountered this type of process story-making world again when I decided to study this method of learning for my doctorate degree at Ohio State University. I worked with Dr. Brian Edmiston, author of *Transforming Teaching and Learning through Active Dramatic Approaches* (2013), about his work with kids, teens, and adults using story-based play.

I spent the next five years working with kids of all ages and adults to co-create and improvise problem-based story work. Edmiston shared models to move the story, using skillful dramatic and educational moves such as *tableaux* and *freeze-frame* to move the investment of the story. These are dramatic methods to illustrate the story in a way that enacts the drama. A tableau creates frozen still images that help the students revisit the story. freeze-frame holds still significant parts of the story so it can be explored more by students' questions. These techniques help the investment in the narrative. Most of all, Edmiston modeled how process-based story work builds inquiry and investment not only in the story but also in the whole group as well.

Later I worked with the legendary Dorothy Heathcote (*Drama for Learning*, 1995) who created a pedagogy entitled *Mantle of the Expert,* a method that uses role to help adults and kids experience a world they create through the eyes of "perceived experts". For example, when I worked with young elementary students in England we engaged in a real world drama of rescuing a wounded adult from a mountain. However, these young children took on the mantle of the expert lens of mountain rescue helpers. I learned the great strength that role has in promoting story development.

On one occasion, a group of fifth graders in Columbus, Ohio struggled with whether or not they should go up the beanstalk to steal the magic coin on top from the giant Jim to help cure their sick mother. I learned how to step into the fictional world with the students to make decisions and use roles such as playing the mother and not only saying I am sick but showing them with my frailty in talking and moving. This helped them become more empathic toward me as their mother.

What is important to know is that this is not a series of dramatic games, but instead, it is using drama and story to help establish framework in the fictional world. Each exercise and convention has been framed to support the world-building that occurs in an ensemble manner.

However I also learned how to have a class discussion outside of the fictional world so we could talk about what we should do and then go back into the fictional world together. These proven techniques can also be employed with writers and storytellers as they step in and out of the world they create.

Another time, using process drama, Edmiston demonstrated the unpredictable and even emotional delivery of suspense. Adults all, and not knowing, we were asked to build a fictional school that would maximize learning for all students. We took out large piece of butcher paper and began to create. Acting in the role of building planners, we carefully chose where to place the library, the classes, and debated issues such as whether or not we would have recess. There was a limitless budget. However, using our fictional power to slowly reveal we were not building an ideal school, but in fact were building a school to strip all Native Americans from their "injun" ways.

This was similar to the real school referred to as the Carlisle school. This school followed these instructions. They used inhumane methods to "naturalize" Native Americans. Our dramatic work mirrored this. Realizing what was occurring, our class had to decide whether to quit and let someone else build this terrible school, or continue to build and work to change it. In the fictional world, we did not know the next direction in building this story. In fact, Edmiston drew upon our compassion for building the best school as educators, and the anger from what was occurring, to determine our next story-based move. It was a dramatic way to shift the story that was being told. I learned how to use power and suspense to build a story. I remember being profoundly affected by this dramatic experience. I could not stop thinking about it. When I wrote an e-mail to Edmiston that night, he responded that my unresolved thinking about the drama shows how powerful drama can be used to help us think or reconsider our actions after the drama. Creating story-based fictional worlds can help us consider what we do in actual time. Drama and story can be reflection tools for continual learning.

Another time, working with teens, we decided to study the causes for the sinking of the Titanic. Students served as reporters immediately after the Titanic sank, interviewing survivors. I used dramatic choices to move the story, but I did not know the outcome. Soon iceberg specialists testified, witnesses described the cold, and parents waited to see if their loved ones came back or suffered in the depths of the water.

In all these cases, I learned how to use play to promote learning. We used role, suspense, perspective, power, and dramatic tension to move in the story world.

This form of play challenged a new understanding of how, as a writer, storyteller, teacher, and imaginative thinker, I could use play. I was left wondering:

1. How could I write in nontraditional ways using play?
2. How would I create stories using play and find new direction for my story work?
3. How could I work with others using play in creating stories?
4. How could I teach differently using play and story?
5. In what way could I increase my imaginative thinking when concentrating on process over product?

In this book, you will discover new ways to work with your story craft and find new story direction using play. Indeed, play is a meaningful way to create and learn.

In both childhood and adult play, the imagination plays a central role in the meaning-making process. Although there are many types of play including school-based, recess, and sports, this work is rooted in play, inviting the writer, storyteller, or imaginative thinker to make choices as they work to create meaning in their work. This play creates a dramatic interface. We use dramatic conventions and world-building to help shape the story we are working on.

I will share how collaborative play can increase your choices when making a story. You will find not only exercises to build your story-making and telling skills, but a pedagogy of practice to use when you are called to create story.

Before you can do any of this, you must first give yourself permission to play. In this world, we have people and places that serve to constrain your use of play. It is powerful when you are reminded daily of the power of play. I value this pledge because it is a strong statement to begin your day as you encounter others who are yet to realize the rich life choices that can be made with play. You can remember this by continuing to take the *Permission 2 Play Pledge*.

Permission 2 Play Pledge
© Kevin D. Cordi

I give myself permission

To have fun.
To take risks.
To make mistakes.
To Play
With my thinking
my choices
my direction and development

to suspend
what I know
so
I know more

I give myself
Permission
To
fail, succeed, and play again.

I have the right to shape
My stories.

I am the crafter and creator.
I am imaginative and supportive

I know through
Play
We understand our stories
And our stories become
alive.

I give myself
Permission to Play.

Chapter 2
What is Story-Crafting?
Exploring How Play can Make the Story

We sometimes need to let go of what we know in order to understand more of what we can know. This chapter is about releasing preconceived notions about the story-making process and the fears that restrict story development.

Countless times, individuals have told me that they became blocked within their stories, unable to find the words to advance. They may often go for weeks, months, or even years feeling immobile and frozen. Sadly, they often let the story go. I invite them to *play with story* when they become blocked. Let me illustrate this with an example.

Play in Texas

It was a calm Texas evening when I was working with the San Antonio Storytelling guild. A woman agreed to play with her story, confiding in me that she felt trapped in its development and wanted to explore more ways to play with the story. The story began in the late 1900s with a young couple's trip across the ocean. To begin, instead of concentrating on her written words, we concentrated on the ship Using what I call *story mediation*, the other storytellers watching the story became active within the story. Story mediation is the careful listening and guiding of story in the present time. We don't talk about the story from the past perspective, but we place ourselves in the time of the story. The storytelling guild members began echoing the sounds of birds that might be heard above the ship and even mirrored the couple's conversations. We heard the bellow of the Captain's orders, the sounds of the ocean waves, and even recreated the moment when the couple first met. Together the ensemble texturized the sound environment of the tale, creating the audio background and inviting the teller to experience the story sounds in addition to telling them. However, by using play we did not work on the story sequentially from one event to the next. Instead, the teller shared that the story followed this couple over time. We began playing with what would happen if the ship were sailing in the thirties, sixties, and even modern times. I remember that one person said, "Was it not a shame that the president was shot?" Or we might hear, "My family has been starving. The stock market crashed and I live nowhere near New York, why do I have to suffer?" This type of play created awareness for the changing times of the story. This awareness was used in the making or crafting the story. After we finished our play, storytellers responded as the couple enacted the writing of letters to each other recounting time lost. People said, "Why have you not written? I have not heard from you since the war broke out?" Others were very specific. "When you met my parents for the first time, my dad thought you were crazy." In the end, the teller felt that this journey through play provided her with new growth of her story.

To move through the story, we focused on significant events, imagining dialogue and developing scenes we could play using the entire group. These intentional conventions invited the teller to consider her story within a larger context. Each listener became a participant and he or she engaged in conversation that we might hear that evoked the time period. Play invited their creativity to freeze story moments and rewind or fast-forward, envisioning new ways to share what we experienced. After over an hour of fruitful, productive play, the teller not only felt she could advance her story, but also decided to rework it using some of the playful methods we employed.

Let me share another way I used play to develop a story:

Walking in Tennessee
I was walking in Jonesborough with a storyteller shortly before the National Storytelling Festival. He said he felt stuck

with his story about the Greek tale of Archne. I asked, "Could we play with story together?" He worried about the tone in his story. We talked about the pacing of the story. After a brief conversation, he and I *walked the story* which invites experiencing the highs and lows through movement. As the story was agitated or the trouble or conflict heightened, we would walk faster. I am sure we looked silly as we slowed down and then sped up walking down the unpaved roads of Jonesborough. With each step, he was finding that Archne did not talk fast, but was deliberate. She was powerful and the teller even punched his foot when talking about her. When the story needed to be calm, he walked slower. However, the impact was heard when Archne entered the story. The changes in pace revealed the internal story rhythm. After our walk, the teller shared that he did not feel frozen anymore and was going to continue to work the rhythm of the story later.

These are only a few directed exercises to help a storyteller, writer, and/or imaginative thinker move story through a commitment to play. On most occasions, when a teller feels stuck in his or her narrative development, he or she may not think differently or in nonconventional ways to invite creativity and innovation. They need to release what they know about story development to explore new ways of discovery. Many forms of exploration may not be directly connected to story. The story-crafter can spend time working on a character and stepping in his or her shoes. Some of what is discovered can be used and proven to be valuable. However, he or she must also explore what might not be valued in order to find the value. Play is about trying out a range of dramatic and story-based choices to discover new awareness.

Story and Writing

Traditionally, in the classroom we exclusively link story and writing. We forget that as children we most likely experienced story by orally talking nonstop about why we thought the sky was so high and why we couldn't touch it. Children would draw their narratives with a big pencil or a box of sixty-four colors. Recess extended story into new worlds of dance, play, or simple narratives. Teachers shared big pieces of butcher paper where we would draw life-size stories at all stages of development. We would laugh at our mistakes, while listening to our friends' suggestions to enhance our stories or even share ownership.

Children share stories and take risks because they are motivated to create story. This is the innocence of childhood. A time when we don't worry about what method to create; we simply create. As adults, we lose this innocence. We can return to a time when we welcomed play, without judgment, as we use various ways to create story. We must agree that it is possible. Although noted friend and colleague, professional storyteller Jay O'Callahan once said to me, "Storytelling is a lonely business," I challenge this notion. When crafting stories, we do not have to be alone. We can invite others to play and experiment with us. However, when we are alone, we often think that writing is our first response to creating stories. We need to dismiss the notion that when we are alone and creating story, we must write it down.

As we age, we may limit our creative options. One example is when we choose writing as the only way to develop story. We edit and change our written copy and after many drafts, decide to finish the story. This is limiting the potential of story. Story has greater reach and depth. It needs to be shaped and reshaped. Writing is one way to explore creating stories, but this craft we know as story can be explored in the same way a potter shapes clay. Starting with an idea is like the raw clay. For story-crafters, who consist of anyone working in the development of stories, their "clay" is the narrative. The form or shape of the narrative is not always understood but through play, many directions can be pursued to help the narrative take shape. However, just as the potter shapes in his act of creation, a storyteller can use many tools, including writing, to mold a story. The story-crafters need to play with the shapes before a final product is created. Examining story as craft, many art forms and methods can be used to create a well-composed narrative. Rosy Greenlees, the Director of the Crafts Council in England defines craft:

> Contemporary craft is about making things. It is an intellectual and physical activity where the maker explores the infinite possibilities of materials and processes to produce unique objects. To see craft is to enter a world of wonderful things which can be challenging, beautiful, sometimes useful, tactile, extraordinary, and to understand and enjoy the energy and care, which has gone into their making. (n.d.)

Storytelling and story writing are essential tools for shaping ideas. As artists, we sometimes forget to explore the infinite possibilities and stop short when cultivating our ideas. Instead of settling on one way to make the story, let us make many stories, or at least story ideas, and use story-crafting tools so that we can understand more the form it will become. Storytellers must tell, but to truly maximize imaginative thinking, should not be limited to one mode of learning, such as writing. When we merge the arts to create story, our craft grows, extends, and is questioned and revealed. We need to draw on a simple plan that fosters our story-making.

First, we develop a plan. This is simply a direction for our stories, not a set firm map that conveys all the roads to crafting a story. Instead, we can work with a simple sketch that outlines the basic directions of a story. By answering a few questions, we can begin. We must first let go of what we know and forget some of our assumptions of story development.

Letting Go of Assumptions

American actor, director, screenwriter, and author Alan Alda says: "Begin challenging your own assumptions. Your assumptions are your windows on the world. Scrub them off every once in a while, or the light won't come in."

Be willing to change your habits. To be creative, we must be mindful in making the choice to break our habits. Play invites novelty, creation, and exploration. We can try different tasks and express new ideas without ridicule. Play experiments without recreating our ordinary life or focusing on our same life choices. We are free to explore new directions and alternative choices. Failure is protected and encouraged. In life, if we fall down, people ignore or rush to help us. In play, you can say "Wait, I need to fall down harder, softer, louder, bolder, brighter," and nobody questions it. In fact, in play, observers can be participants in your play. They can help you establish the best sound when you fall and how you can do it again, but with even more finesse. We question when this happens in real time. In playtime, it is not questioned. There is freedom in play and we need to explore this freedom when we craft stories.

Play as a Constructive Tool for Storytelling

Play can be scheduled time not to practice something already created; instead, it is a time designated to explore new directions. In V. Glasgow

Koste's book, *Dramatic Play in Childhood: Rehearsal for Life* (1995), play is defined as a time for "rehearsal for life." I don't see play as rehearsal for what is occurring, but instead, practice and reflection of the possibilities that could arise out of the play. Instead of a mirror for life, it is more an undefined map of possibilities. Play is not practice for real time and doesn't rely on what is, but what could be. Creative impulses don't always occur in the everyday, but instead in the possible. The strongest words in play are *I wonder, imagine,* and *what if.* What is even stronger is when you lead with the word *we.* "I wonder what would happen if we ..." "Imagine if we lived during the medieval ages." "What would happen if we were the discoverers of gravity?" Even stronger is when those words are more than words but instead serve as a platform for creating places to play. Words and actions are brought to life by playing out an action, movement, or design.

Play challenges the writer or storyteller to question his or her ordinary habits used to create ideas. Habits can in fact narrow our choices. If we take the same road to work every day, we know the road and only that road. Breaking from routine, we might be introduced to the fall foliage or the twelve point buck that crosses a new road Play invites different roads and different vehicles to get there. Writing for many can be the same road. Writing is not the only way to create. Narrative play invites new directions. Playing out loud can enable a highway of choices instead of a single path.

Why shouldn't we try something new to challenge our creativity? When you sit at the computer typing, you can create a story script. The script may not be ready. Spoken word exercises can create a variety of choices before cementing words on paper. Let the words take shape by trying out the spoken exercises instead of practicing them with a pen, pencil or keyboard. Spend more time imagining possibilities for the story before creating a script. Try playing with the ideas, moments, sounds and the contrasting tensions, changing the endings and the beginnings. Find a partner or a group with whom to share these ideas. All dimensions of stories can be subjects of play. As story-crafters, we can work with one single moment in a story or even extend an attitude that is in a story. All this work can develop better stories.

The Habits we Need to Release to Invite Play

Let go of old habits used when crafting stories. Let go of always writing stories down as the only way to create. Let go of always starting at the beginning and working until the end. Don't forget that we are taught in school that stories begin by creating plot. These habits are ingrained and must be challenged to study new ways of crafting story. William James said, "All our life, so far as it has definite form, is but a mass of habits,—practical, emotional, and intellectual,—systematically organized for our weal or woe, and bearing us irresistibly toward our destiny, whatever the latter may be." (James 1925) In turn, this same set of habits should be suspended in order to engage in play.

The Power of Habit (2012) by Charles Duhigg cites a research study conducted at Duke University concluding, "more than 40 percent of the actions people performed each day weren't actual decisions, but habits" (xvi). Duhigg defines habits as, "… the choices that all of us deliberately make at some point, and then stop thinking about but continue doing, often every day" (xvii). This work invites individuals to release established story development habits or at least question them to reveal new ways of making and working with stories. Instead, we need to explore story development that might at first be unfamiliar or even uncomfortable. This approach is new and different. It challenges the status quo. The unfamiliar can be daunting. As writer W. Somerset Maugham reminds us, "The world in general doesn't know what to make of originality; it is startled out of its comfortable habits of thought, and its first reaction is one of anger" (1948 136). People may balk at the uneasiness of working in this frame. However, one must work to be comfortable with tension. I argue tension is not unproductive. I have found, after working with hundreds of people, that tension is the agent that creates new direction. After all, how often have you felt a little on edge and it made you rethink or even take a new action? In play, tension can be the thing that moves you to reconsider your actions or even aggravate them. Tension is different than fear. Tension is when you feel on edge but are able to explore. Fear can paralyze you and keep you from moving forward. "To him who is in fear everything rustles." —Sophocles, playwright.

Letting Go of Fear

When we are in school, parents, teachers, and fellow students perceive us as being brave because we shared a story or idea out loud in class. Teachers and adults marvel when students have learned all those lines in a play and couple it by announcing that he or she could never do it because they are too afraid. Teachers say, "Who is brave enough to go first?" We are called up to speak in front of the class and we begin to form a mindset that talking out loud or sharing in public is something to be feared. This mindset can stunt creativity, exploration, and discovery.

We need to let go of fear. In *Feel the Fear and Do It Anyway* (1987), author Susan Jeffers shared that underlying our fears is lack of trust in ourselves. Fear can both cripple and fuel creativity. Fear invites exploration of unknown choices to develop our narratives. With story work, the risk is manageable. No one is asked to jump into shards of broken glass or be humiliated because he or she is not prepared. Instead, play helps establish a safe environment for risk taking. Fear and risk are intertwined. As the English bard William Shakespeare reminds us, "Our doubts are traitors, and make us lose the good we oft might win by fearing to attempt." Fear can paralyze, rendering us helpless in our choices. When we realize our choices are meant to be fearful and risky, we can accept new developments in our work. Fear will surface in many ways and identification is key. Play is one way to deal with fear.

Let go of fear of the unknown. Play is about exploring the unknown. The more one explores the unknown, the more comfortable the mystery will become. Unknown directions help build stronger connections. I remember when I was in California, one hundred and eighty-three students hosted a Tellabration, a national night of storytelling that occurs all over the world at the same time. I had six professional storytellers waiting to tell. We didn't have time for all of them. I instead quickly shared that we could all tell a version of the southern story "Old Drye Frye" and soon after, the professionals took the stage. I naturally assumed everyone knew this story. They did not. It was a southern story, and I was in California. Instead of panicking, we enchanted the audience of four hundred listeners to a new tale of "Old Drye Frye" as he sailed into space, met new friends, and came back alive and choked on a chicken bone, again. Our happy accident became a delight of a tale. The unfamiliar did not become our fear. We embraced it and told our tale. Audrey Flack, famous painter and sculptor, said, "If you can't paint, paint Big". This is the proper spirit when it comes to fear and risk. Take chances, and be "Big" when working in play. It is important to remember the mere fact that the work within play does not have to perfect.

Let go of fear of rejection, be open to trust. When directing the National Youth Storytelling Olympics—now called Showcase—a nine-year-old girl arrived late to perform for an audience of seventeen-hundred people. Well known teller Bobby Norfolk was prepared to perform as a substitute. I was emceeing and immediately wanted Camille to know that if she did not feel ready, she didn't have to perform. I looked out to the sea of over a thousand faces and knew this could be intimidating. In a giant tent with a thousand adults from all walks of life, I was sure she was nervous.

I will never forget her response. She tightened her little hat, looked at the audience, and said, "Mr. Cordi, those people are there for me and I am not going to turn them down." She received not one, but two standing ovations. This is the way we need to see the performance of our stories for audiences. When we perform, it is not always for us, but also for our audience. In my over twenty-eight years as a professional storyteller and writer, witnessing thousands of people watching others perform or read their stories, not once have I heard a myriad of boos or disgust. It is easily forgotten that performance is a safe place. Instead, we allow an old school misrepresentation of speaking aloud or performing to create fear. This outdated mindset can alter our direction. We need to change this, and the best way we can do this is to acknowledge the possible presence of fear, but remember that we are working for a bigger cause than the fear. We want to share our work with the world.

As writers, storytellers, or other imaginative thinkers, we craft our work to share later. This is not to say that we don't create for ourselves. When we hear a story, we listen to how we can connect with it. When we are working on a story, we connect to our experiences. It helps us remember that the story is more than its words. We need to continue to seek these connection points, seeing the possibilities in the story-making process. Shifting fear to sharing possibilities with an audience is not an easy transition. Telling a story makes the teller vulnerable by sharing their words and performance. Each successful performance—and, there will be many—reduces fear. Telling and writing stories to be vocally shared is a unique exchange among teller, listener, and audience. The success of this connected exchange depends on the link among the three.

Stories as Gifts

We need to enter the world of story performance in the same way as we present gifts. In casual conversation, Lance Hansen, Cheyenne storyteller and poet shared, "Stories are gifts; it is up to us to take them or receive them."

Instead of concentrating on what might go wrong and fearing rejection, the power of story transformation is a unique gift that only the teller can deliver. Storytelling audiences welcome tellers. Fear should not override your telling. Let the story be presented as the gift you share. Trust your work. Trust in the audience's willingness to listen. Trust that the unique connection works. It does.

Let go of fear of judgment. If the teller walks on stage and only thinks of the audience as a pack of judges equipped with negative feedback of their work, he or she will only experience fear of the performance. Others may provide nonconstructive feedback of your work, but this should not hold you back. Inexperienced listeners of story will judge you based on the one or two storytellers they have heard. However, these people will be in the minority. Still a greater number will thank you for telling a story that helped them remember their grandmother, laugh with Brer Rabbit again, or simply enjoy a live performance. The listener too can be drawn to other places through your story and therefore evaluates the experience via their experience. You can't always be responsible for the journey of the listener. Listen to everyone's responses to your story.

Always remember during a performance, the audience will be listening and sharing in the experience with you. The time to hear that judgment is later. Sometimes the criticism is asked for and warranted, but others times provided without asking. This book does not concentrate on polished, performance-ready work, but rather focuses on stories that are not ready for performance but are ready for play to further explore the craft. Stories are formed, mistakes are made, and in play this is accepted. Let go of the audience judging you. Instead, see them as co-creators of the work. In this, the listeners can be active agents helping your story take shape. However, this co-creation explores choices not directed by evaluative rules or stipulations. Instead, the audience becomes aware of your work and how you are playing with its creation. They serve to help you see it in new ways and explore new directions. In the end, you own the story and you control the changes you want to accept or deny.

Let go of the fear of looking stupid. Play supports exploration that can appear crazy, silly, alive and aware. We are encouraged to act on choices, and to question and seek understanding. Constraints are suspended to explore new ideas. In the world of play, real world restrictions can fade. Let me illustrate with an example.

> During my study at Ohio State University, I engaged in play with elementary students. Together with the teacher Mitch, and later my advisor Brian Edmiston, I worked with four second grade urban children who were blind. One student also had cerebral palsy. They were interested in exploring Mars, and for four weeks, we used story-crafting and dramatic play to create a mission. From this experience, I saw how students could use play to step into roles they could not necessarily hold in their real lives. In other dialogic inquiry story-based experiences, I had seen students step into the roles of German children during the Berlin airlift, African American pilots, students attending Houdini's séances, and engineers on the Titanic. We used story-crafting and drama and made the impossible possible. Students who were blind saw in the fictional world. With these four students, we built a spaceship and used clay models and Brailers to communicate with Martians.
>
> When we landed, the students created cosmic dust that clouded the adults' eyes while shielding the students who were the astronauts. This left the adults blind so the blind students volunteered to lead us. In the real world, these were blind students walking into a classroom; but in the fictional world they were experienced, seeing astronauts leading their temporarily blind teammates around the planet Mars. It was here that I saw how the use of play provided students more than a voice to speak. It gave them a world to see. Using play, I watched students ask questions about Mars, such as, its size and ability to sustain life for these second graders. They wanted to know how Martians could survive. In the fictional world, being blind was not a deterrent to preparing and visiting Mars.

In this ensemble work, the students did not worry about looking stupid, but rather with making their world real. They did not let the fact that they were blind or small stop them from preparing and traveling to Mars.

When we let go of how we think, look or behave, we can explore our choices and believe in the worlds we create. Only then can we play and feel safe about our wise and not so wise choices that we make together. We need to remember that individual fears become the group's fears. In order to play, we need to work not from a point of fear, but from discovery. With this mindset, possibilities abound.

Narratives are Meant to be Messy

There are a number of story concepts that need to be broken to be able to play with story. Writers and storytellers need to open possibilities when they work with narrative. Narrative is meant to be messy (Ochs and Capps 2001). It is in the disentanglement of narrative when tension rises. When tension is used in play, more choices can be explored. Imagine trying to tell the story of "Little Red Riding Hood" within these changing conventions. The wolf suddenly interrupts the narrative to share his side of the story. At the same time, we hear Red's mother chime in. At the same time, we hear Little Red's innocent voice as she tries to make sense of what happens only to be broken by the grandmother exclaiming how she had warned Little Red about the dangers of the woods. Imagine the delightful tangled up narratives yet to be discovered for story development from these voices. Suspending traditional storytelling methods for creative play deepens the playful choices. Playing outside of the box with story development helps create direction.

It is Time to Consider Story Concepts as We Engage in Play.

Story occurs in chronological order. As most improvisers know, story begins in the middle. The middle of the action is where new stories can take new directions. If we are confined to the structure of exclusively working from the beginning to restructure, we can be stuck with only working from there. However, this is not a realistic way for story-crafters to work their art. Ask any writer if he or she begins writing the first page and ends with the last page. Most almost never do this. Even in writing this book, ideas came in various stages. From walking down the street and thinking or deliberating talking out loud, I found new direction for the book. This is more similar to how writers compose. They answer to the pulse of what is necessary, or they simply want to experiment when they write. They might spend a day on a character, another day changing the environment, and the next day working on something that is not fleshed out in the work. However, some schools teach us an artificial way to create story. The story sequence taught in school is modeled from the idea that we write stories as they occur from the beginning to the end. When teachers coach, they look at the fact that it is not finished, as this is the part they need to work on, not seeing what was already developed. They rarely look at the brainstorming or outline notes, which I would argue, are great starting points for playing with story. They instead look for a plot. Teachers are plot-driven when providing instruction on how to create a story. A little girl who is lost in the woods and finds a wolf, is not exciting. However, it is the plot of "Little Red Riding Hood." Why not start in the middle, when the wolf first discovers Red? Why can't students write about the large teeth that serve as markers of the impending doom and the fear that Red has when she sees the teeth moving closer to her. This is not a plot point, but instead a moment of action. Here we can play with the action and see what happens. Instead, we start at the beginning. To make it worse, we often ask students to generate plot before experimenting with choices that they could make creating the action of the story.

In play, we can hold the order still. Instead of working on the chronological order of "Little Red Riding Hood", we can stay with the time that Little Red is explaining to the wolf her reasons for traveling to grandmother's house and why she must arrive soon. If we use play here in the story, we can flesh out more choices in the story. Perhaps Red is the type of girl that wonders about everything, leading to why she asks, "Why grandmother has big eyes … teeth." By holding this moment still, we can explore why the wolf feels the need to trick the girl and swallow her whole. In play, the wolf can explain how he needs little girls for his new diet craze or one can discover that perhaps in the past Red tricked the wolf. The imaginative possibilities help direct the story and are not guided by some artificial sense of order that we learned from outdated school practices. Again, the possibilities for working with story open for us when we neglect chronological order.

Work on the entire story from beginning, middle, and end. When working with story, sometimes it is most effective to work with a specific action in a story or the way a character behaves. At this point, this is the focus for playing and not working with the entire story. Instead of seeing a story as something that must have a beginning, middle, and end, view it as a series of episodes. A television episode of *Cheers, Mash, Friends* or *The Big Bang Theory* did not always connect to another episode but instead captured a full moment during the episode. These single events can be enough material to develop an idea further. We can simply work on a single moment such as when Little Red first discovers she is lost and find out more about why she is lost.

We can even examine the mood of the hunter when he discovers the wolf. Moments with the story can be broken down to highlight pockets of time or episodic events. For example, we can even play with creating something that happens to the character that is not in the story we are composing. We can create a backstory to explore the depth of the character. We might play with the idea that the wolf has been abandoned by his pack and this is why he is a big bad wolf. We might enact the first time Little Red has to act like a grown-up because her grandmother needs her. Each episode might make the story plot or environment more vivid without ever being connected to plot. In some cases, episodes may appear to have no connection, but through exploration, the choices discovered inform the story later in the development. Actors explore their characters, even traveling for days behaving in role.

Written script must be retold. Too often we use a script in story-crafting. We believe a written text must be used and the script must be what we retell to improve the story already written. Actors are anchored in the script as they practice and perform. Written scripts handcuff us and limit our choices. Some storytellers, writers, and other imaginative thinkers would never think of deviating from the script. As writers, we cling to the written work first and feel we must stay with our words as we transition to telling. Some storytellers scribe first only, then work within the written frame they created. We need to learn to scatter the script to the winds to find new directions, wrestling with our choices through using different modes and styles. Find a group or partner to play with stories orally and only after this work, cement it in print—this is only if we feel the need to have a typed script. After working with the story orally, both storytellers and writers will find their written copy has more range. Storytellers will discover through this exploration that their range of choices expands and diversifies.

Avoid the fear of letting others view our work while it is in process. Finally, story-crafters should let go of the myth that if someone is watching us work with a story, he or she will ridicule our work. Instead, we need to reposition how we see those who help us play with our stories as story-crafters.

Listeners can provide new perspectives that give our stories new life.

> I was working on a story from Azerbaijan titled "The Peace Dove." I performed it for other people and invited suggestions. As it happened two people that heard this tale were from this war-torn country. They began to share the way their parents told them a version of this story as a child, how menacing the Sultans in the story could sound, and how peaceful the ending was for them. One man revealed that he saw the beginning starting from a dream. They shared how they experienced the story. We played with the ideas together, and I was able to create a better story from their suggestions.

> Another time, I worked with a group of teenagers exploring why the Titanic sank, and instead of talking about it, together we created a story-based world where we could explore from multiple perspectives what happened. Soon students, as "specialists," began to research the strength of the ice. Some became the voice of the Captain and some became passengers, and we were able to build empathy for the story we were telling together. However, we were also able to freeze certain times, including the instant when the ship was struck, how the Captain first found out that he was to man the great ship, and the newspaper headlines that were read after the event. Afterwards, the students did not view this event as something passive, but instead actively asked questions about the day the ship sank. As we used play, their inquiry grew, and their questions became more unresolved. We collectively worked together to explore how the ship sank, what type of man the Captain was, and even imagined the conversations on the ship. This was a rich experiential history lesson made active and alive. We built more than an understanding of the facts of this awful time, but built empathy for those involved.

These episodes may help form the backbone of the story, or as Vi Hilbert, an elder of the Skagit of the greater Puget Salish in Washington State, once shared with me at the Bay Area Storytelling Festival, "the skeleton of the story". However, once we have the skeleton, we need to add more flesh to the story. When we practice stories, we often tell the stories from beginning to end. This is effective for stories deemed ready or finished—although I would argue that play can be used at any time for stories. In play, we are not confined to rules. The play is not constrained by working in chronological time, in a specific order, or from a written script. Instead, work from the episodes that help the story develop and become familiar. Play makes a story ready to be seen and experienced.

Preparing to Work with Play—It Begins with Breathing

I have found that in order to let go of these habits and assumptions, it first it becomes necessary to prepare the mind and the body for the work of play, to be in a state of readiness. Nothing prepares a creative artist better than breathing.

After returning from Japan in 2001, I examined life through a calmer window. In Japan, there was stillness. A taxi driver walked me to a restaurant on foot so I would not be lost or late. I saw a quiet appreciation for nature and the strange chaos of the Japanese fish market. Initially it appeared chaotic, but when I looked again, I witnessed children learning commerce, fish cleaning skills, and how to communicate with each other from their older mentors. Despite the blaring of the horns, the massive number of people running into the market and the sharp distinct fish smell, the place was quiet, restorative, and memorable.

I saw older Japanese quietly, not forcefully, teaching young children to clean fish. I weaved these ideas into my teaching, my storytelling, and in my work with play.

Could this simplicity be used to help create stories? Why do our brains race with our bodies? The Buddhist practice of slowing down is called, *mindfulness.* Although I am not a practicing Buddhist, I do strive for mindfulness. I believe this work can help us improve story development.

Why Should we Concentrate on Breathing? As Ruth Sawyer, author of *The Way of the Storyteller* (1942) states,

> Let the first concern be about the breath. Learn to breathe from below the belt, not superficially from the chest. Learn to control the breath by the abdominal muscles, not the throat muscles … whether one speaks correctly or not, for general health, for keeping one's voice strong, free, and untiring, one should work regularly at this matter of proper breathing. (134)

Most communication theorists and researchers agree that up to seventy percent of all communication depends on how we breathe. However, as writers and storytellers we spend little time concentrating or practicing our breathing because we think something else is more important. I contend nothing can be done without first breathing well. Whether I am telling stories or presenting story-based programs to young children or senior citizens, we breathe with each program. I make every attempt to have my audience and/or participants breathe with me between and sometimes during the stories.

For the teller—Often we feel rushed, impulsive or even apprehensive when starting a storytelling session or program. The same is true when we begin to develop story programming. Release the tension by breathing to slow down. Breathing with intent not only slows us down, but also places us in the moment of story invitation. This is where, as a teller, you focus on the way you begin and visualize the telling with the audience.

For the listener—When you include times for the audience to breathe with you, they follow the story with the rate that allows them to quickly visualize the story. Following are exercises that I have used to help with breathing.

Breathing Techniques to Help Story-Crafting.

These techniques can be used with youth and adults for story-making and telling.

1. *Reflect on breathing.* For five full minutes, invite writers, storytellers, or other imaginative thinkers to simply focus on their breathing. Do they breathe fast or slow? Do they breathe where their shoulders rise—chest breath—or from their stomach—diaphragmatic breathing? Do they rush their mind thinking of other things or simply concentrate on their breathing? Do they relax or are they agitated when they breathe?

2. *Practice diaphragmatic breathing.* Place one hand on your stomach and breathe so your shoulders do not rise. If it does not immediate happen, don't worry. Don't force it. Concentrate on making it so. When you do, you will be using your diaphragm when breathing and this will not only increase lung strength, but also body and mind strength as well.

3. *Softly count while non-forcibly exhaling.* As practice each day, you should count in slow deliberate tones as you exhale. Each day on your own time, practice increasing the duration of each exhale when breathing. However, do not

force the exhale—this will be very harmful. Instead, work on gradually increasing the count. This will provide more breath resonance and therefore strengthen your energy level.

4. *Visualize your story during your breathing.* As you become accustomed to breathing, visualize the story while you count. Do not rush. Allow your breathing to let you see the story. Initially, start with the whole story, and then when you are comfortable, you can select certain episodes in the story to visualize.

5. *Once you try these four steps, adapt breathing in your telling.* Now that you have worked with these steps, you can adjust your breathing. Pay particular attention to possible silence or pausing that you can use for your story. You will find your whole story manner has a better sense of control. You are now allowing the story to take shape to compliment your breathing. Practice this and you will develop a new sense of awareness in telling

Each time you practice effective breathing exercises your success in play will grow.

Working with Different Forms and Modes

As discussed, we often refer to writing as the only mode that our stories can take as we engage in play. We can also play with other modes such as painting, drawing, and acting. These modes should be employed only after working with story, using play methods outlined in the subsequent chapters. They are listed here to as other ways to experience story. I challenge you to practice your story using these modes. The practice can occur simply from an idea. You use different modes to explore or play with an idea or it can occur after you have told the story and you want to see it in a new light. By playing with these modes, you can envision your story differently and often discover new directions for your story. Note that these modes can occur at any time during story-crafting.

New Modes to use When Story-Crafting

We need to discover story by experiencing it outside of its written form. Considering the weight of these words, when our craft is story, we can mix the modes and mediums that we use to understand our craft. There is a difference between using the arts to understand the craft of story and studying the arts to become experts. In this work, you are encouraged to step out of your comfort zones to include different modes and mediums. From drawing an image or composing a melody to experimenting with words, the story can again move in new directions. As story-crafters, we must not be limited to one mode or practice to find ideas. Below are other ways that can help story-crafters discover their story in a new frame.

Drawing—How often, instead of writing the story, have you instead drawn it? I recently talked with my colleague at Ohio Dominican University, Dr. Jessica Larva. She has a degree in drawing and stated that she often refers to drawing stick people to make a point. She said the simple act of drawing can help you see what you want to say. Take some unlined paper and draw significant moments in your story. The key is to provide as much detail in the image as possible.

Image and Symbolic Search—Imagine if you scoured magazines or the Internet for images to retell the story. The choices you make will help you think about the story in a new way. The images can symbolically represent the story. Details can come from other images. Another way is to find shapes that tell the story. You can even find shapes to create an emotional effect and demand on the visual viewer.

Cartoon—Create a storyboard and share the story as a comic strip Recently my students studied anti-bullying using visual literacy. They composed comic strips that highlighted perspective, positioning, bold text choices, and strong images. They told effective educational stories from the images. Again, don't worry about being an award-winning cartoonist. Instead, use the frame to revisit your story ideas. When the work is revisited in the shape of cartoons, only the essential elements can be shared. This can help story-crafters recognize the essential and nonessential in the story.

Dancing—Movement can create direction and especially, empathy for story. I once worked with a choreographer who created a dance based on a short story idea. She was able to show physically how the story communicated. Working with movement is a valuable way of re-imagining the development of the story.

Finger paint, clay or even Play Dough™—When you mold the story, you can see, in concrete form, significant times in the story. Once again, work the detail into each form. You will be surprised at how this can help the story to take shape—pun intended.

Puppetry—I have a friend and colleague who is not only an internationally touring storyteller but also puppeteer. Randel McGee showed me how by using puppets, we can with express a narrative in a way that gives new voices to the tale. By speaking with and through a puppet, the story can become a dialogue, which can help explore the way voice is used in the story you are creating. You can find out more about Randel's work at http://mcgeeproductions.com

Theater—creating a play. Consider writing a short play from the story. You might write about an episode or two and be surprised by the reactions of the character. When you have to write dialogue, you see the character in a new way. When you see the work in performance, other actors might represent what you say differently but still communicate the message you wanted to deliver. Or they might find a new way to say it.

Poetry—Crafting with poems helps one form new structure. Pick an episode, character, emotional choice, or even the environment and compose a poem. In order to see the work with more depth, consult poetry books about new forms to help generate the work. I recently worked with former Children's Poet Laureate J. Patrick Lewis, who uses poetry to revisit a narrative. He showed me how exploring poetry genre—Haiku, Ballad, the Bop—can help one revisit a story.

Journal—Writing down reactions of the story-crafting process in a journal can provide you with written guidelines to use when creating the story later.

Song—Like poetry, song will force you to view and present your story within a new structure. Well-known story singers like Bill Harley and John McCutcheon compose songs from narrative events. We can learn a great deal when we write a song from the stories we create.

Prepare Yourself for the Next Chapter

After examining how to develop story-crafting with play, letting go of fears, and examining new forms that contain the story, we are ready to explore words in the next chapter. A storyteller or writer's craft depends on words. The next chapter will show you how to make the words dance. Word dancing is a subtle and not so subtle way to play with language to help the story move.

This is a secret, listen close: 'Words can dance; words can jiggle; words can jump 'Words can dive and words can fly; words have movement. 'Words are the tools of a storyteller and writer.

—KEVIN CORDI

Chapter 3
Word Dancing—Proven Playful Methods to Use Before Writing Down Stories

Words are not the only tools. Story-crafters can use imaginative play to help words dance. In this chapter, we explore methods to use words without writing them down. We explore how sharing the words out loud can provide more effective choices for writers, storytellers, and other imaginative thinkers.

Recently, I informally interviewed a number of storytellers—and writers—and discovered that many, almost all, refer to a written text when initially working on a story. The tellers will create a typed script. The script can be arranged from plot points to full stories. They start their development relying on print. One storyteller says "I depend on the writing to move the story," and another confided she would rather type than share it with someone as close as her husband when she is first creating her tale. She said that "He was too close," and that she needed to work first. He would see it only when it was performed. She echoed that this is the method with which she felt most comfortable. I argue, we need to step out of our comfort zones and agree to play with story with or without a script.

The first stage of story development invites play, because at that point, nothing has been decided about the story. We can add new characters, change the environment, introduce conflict, and even scrap it and begin anew. At this stage, there are endless possibilities for story. But often, if even out of habit, we resign ourselves to write it down and hold fast to a script or text when creating our first work. There is nothing wrong with writing down a story or creating a text and working from it. It is one method used to remember the ideas, words, and significant moments of the story. It captures, in a more solid way, the story's direction. However, it is one way and there are many others. In addition to this, I personally support that if we need to write it down, we do this later, and only after we played with other choices. Think of speeches you have heard. You could tell, when the speaker read from the paper containing the speech and never looked at the audience, when you heard it. However, when a speech sounded and felt like genuine expression of the speaker's thoughts and feelings, you knew that the speaker had played with the words. The best orators have practiced their words out loud. They have moved away from their written texts, and have talked out loud to themselves or to someone else before delivering their speeches.

Talking Out Loud

Talking out loud means the speaker, writer, or storyteller is not worried about the exact words to use in their address, but instead focuses orally on the impact of the words. The speaker is aware not only of the dynamics and strength of his or her voice, but also examines how his or her body reacts to the voice. The talking out loud creates a sensory experience. The sound creates a dynamic episode. These episodes become effective markers to determine how it will be received by a live audience. Talking out loud is more natural than writing words on paper, allowing the organic talk experience to happen more efficiently. The natural course of conversation can change at any turn. When a teller, writer, or other imaginative thinker talks out ideas or even episodes of a story, they begin to create not just one experience, but many experiences to use when building a story together. In the talking out loud, the story-crafter does not worry about the logical order, but instead explores a range of spoken choices. They play with the words. They play with the reactions from the words. Talking out loud in the form of verbal exercises is an organic and natural method of play to be valued and woven into our story-crafting. Words can dance, sway, and fly. It is a freeing of the experience when crafting a story. Invite choices that create this freedom.

Writing Before Telling

When story-crafters write their words down, this becomes the frame upon which revisions are based. In turn, when the story-crafter practices this story for a live audience, he or she works from the established lines. However, in play, and in one minute, he or she can explore a new direction without considering an audience. As they talk out loud, they might want to talk about the weather that occurred the night before. There is no judge in play. No one is going to question if it is connected. In play, the story choices can relate, but they don't have to. Once play exercises are established, the story-crafter will have the freedom to roam to various unexplored directions in his or her story. Once these words are written, it is hard to explore other directions. We need to ask, "Is this story ready to be in print? Can I use oral exercises to help see the story differently than I see it now?"

Why Talk Stories Out Loud before Writing Them Down?

Talking is a comfortable place for discovery. It is as natural as breathing. In fact, writing is not as common as talking. Why is it, when it comes to being creative as writers and storytellers, that we go to an unnatural place such as a desk and pen or a keyboard? When we write, we try to make our stories speak. An effective writer uses silence and the environment to create effects. However, most writers create worlds where characters speak out loud. Why not practice out loud to find these voices? Why not practice out loud to find how a teller wants the story to be told? Why not use the natural act of talking out loud to discover story development?

The Spoken Voice is a Goal of all Writers

Our first language is oral (Davis, 2000). We speak before we write. It is how we first communicate as children, but it is also how our story characters communicate. Whether we are writing or telling a story, we are often trying to recapture a scene that is lively and active. We write as though the characters are involved in a conversation with a myriad of other people. In a real sense, we are trying to recreate spoken conversations or stories on paper. Spoken word play is more than playing with how a character sounds, but instead is a methodology used to develop story-crafting. It is a form of word acrobatics or word dancing used to examine what is around, within, and excluded from story. However, with these exercises, one can examine possible choices for the story.

For example, if I intend to create a mystery story, I can orally play with the various voices of each character in the narrative. I can also explore how the sound of the voice of each character helps determine the identity of that character. One can explore by hearing the story aloud how he or she would react to another character as they dramatically recreate the environment that forms the basis for the sound. I can heighten the tension and actually hear how it sounds when shots are fired and then explore the reactions to the sound. This is what happens when we focus out loud on the sounds in a story. I can also work with the environment, another character, tension and more. The exercises require imaginative work, but also the willingness to explore more of the stories as an oral changing text. The text develops when we play out loud, and stories emerge from our word dancing. All of these choices can flow effortlessly when engaged in oral exercises. Although it takes some initial training and releasing of any inhibitions, it is fruitful work. We need to take oral risks to see the ideas build to create a memorable story.

Writing can be a Productive Practice

It is not to say that in revising writings, significant progress cannot be made with the story. However, playing and crafting stories orally can uncover more choices and subsequently lead to a better written script text. A script in this sense is a written record that has all or most of the events in the story outlined in print. A typed structure becomes the framework around which the story revolves. Changes are often made only within that structure. Play can still happen in the revisions, but often can be limited. For example, if a story-crafter is writing a ghost story, they have established the context of the work. In print, they already know when the ghost will appear, what signs announce arrival of the ghost, and even how the story will end. They feel obligated to the written plot points. Changes are made but often within the inherent structure that outlines the ghost's arrival and departure.

Perhaps instead of writing it down, in oral play or what I call word dancing, the exercise can easily shift to spending time talking out loud. The story-crafter can develop the story further working with sounds until the dramatic action creates the desired effect. They don't have to follow the script but can still explore, what does the ghost sound or look like? Why is the ghost hanging around and whom does he haunt? From word dancing, many choices can be explored for one action.

Closer Examination of Word Dancing

Let us look at what happens when someone dances. Why would people move their body in an unnatural way? What logical reason explains why people dance? It is simple. The dance means more. It is a way for dancers to take risks and exhibit uncontrollable freedom to discover something new. With each dance, new meaning is experienced. The way that a body moves leads a person to see and experience all these things in a new way. It creates still and rapid movements that evoke a different feeling, and when this movement is combined, a sense of wonder is made. Nobody's dance experience is the same.

As the African proverb suggests, "When the music changes, so does the dance." Working within play changes the dance, and our dance is story. In this chapter I would suggest—as storytellers, writers, and other imaginative thinkers—our craft is story and that we are word dancers of that craft. As careful choreographers of words, we want words to accompany our meaning-making. With each subtle and not so subtle move, we develop awareness. When our combination of play is experienced, we see the wonder.

The Importance of Practice

To dance well, one must practice the art. Dancers may endure countless rehearsals with an ensemble, but they also practice their craft alone. They will experiment and try many combinations to understand the dance. The dancer might choose to study a specific technique or practice an entire dance. All this practice is merited. It might not bring the dancer to certainty all the time, but it brings clarity. In other words, dancers are not always looking to fully understand the dance. They often dance to explore new methods. Storytellers and writers need to dance without knowing all the steps of the story. Instead, they let their bodies and voices speak out loud to make a big sound. Dancers actively reflect on their work before, during and after their work. Story-crafters should always be in a state of reflection.

As word dancers, we can gain discovery through print, but now that we have agreed to let go of fear, practice good breathing techniques, and be in a state of play, it is time to dance with the words.

Remember, word dancers' tools for play are words and the body. They engage in oral exercises, consciously working to expand story work, by practicing with or without someone else's help, to develop story. Reflection is the key. The storyteller/writer invests in contemplation before the work, in the moment, and after the work.

The Challenge

It is important to note the following exercises can be considered before or after a story is scribed. For the purpose of this chapter, I challenge the reader to complete these exercises first by yourself. Consider initially trying these exercises alone to better understand yourself and how you can work individually with the exercises before asking someone to help. Examine the little and big things such as the sound of your breathing and the versatile work within your voice and body. In many cases, this is untapped knowledge and ability. Only by taking the time to learn about yourself can you know how to listen and work with others.

Once the story-crafter is comfortable with these exercises alone, invite partnership and group work. Step out of a comfortable zone and work with the exercises until they become comfortable choices. When this is established, the story-crafter can be versatile with how and when they are used.

Story-crafters do not traditionally employ these exercises. Once learned, these exercises will provide story-crafters with more tools for building better stories. I have worked with many guilds and storytelling organizations and they often rely solely on coaching with another partner to determine when a story is complete. Coaching is not as common as telling. I challenge story-crafters to experiment orally to enrich their methods when playing with story. The reason I ask you to try this alone first is because, again, this is not common practice. There are times as writers, storytellers, and other imaginative thinkers that we must conduct our business from inside a hotel room or between performances. Much of our work can be solitary. It would be efficient and effective to have oral word dancing exercises to use in these times. There will be times when a computer or even a pen is not available—even though I suggest you have a writing utensil at all times—you will be alone with time and space. One might think this is a lonely time. Lonely is a mindset we need to change. Instead,we need to see this time and space as vital to our discovery. It is a time we can safely play and take risks as we work to discover by ourselves our own understanding of story.

One might have questions about talking out loud and working with oral exercises. I have addressed some of them here.

1. *How long do I work alone when working with my story?* This is not something you work out of; you are not working so you can do partner work after you work by yourself. There is value in both experiences. Both are tools, working orally by yourself helps you discover the improvisational nature that resides in you. Working by yourself, with a partner, and even with a group—I will detail—later creates different focal points. For now, learn the value of talking out loud and listening to what you have to say, verbally and nonverbally when you are in the state of creating.

2. *When will you know you are ready to have a partner?* It is important to understand the work in context of what you and the story need. There are times when working alone will initially help you more than working with a partner. For example, working alone can help you deal with the silences in your story and invite comfort with the rhythm and delivery of the tale. When working with someone else, you might be more aware of the fact that you are telling to a partner instead of placing all your energy into working on the silences. When you work alone with the oral exercises, you don't have to explain them to anyone else. This work can be an amazing place for rehearsal without judgment. You can laugh out loud at what you think are funny ideas to develop and expand your first thoughts. Playing with ideas with another person changes the focus to expand beyond the self-discovery for deep listening and active participation in the play.

3. *Can you work with a partner first and then work by yourself?* Story emerges at all stages of development. These oral exercises can even be used in live performance with stories that are deemed ready. With my story, "Mama's Last Puppy," I have worked with the rhythm for years. This story is set. I might change it every time I tell it, but it is within the structure from a rigid or set structure. Working with play can help you to free an established story. The exercises create a mindset that invites play even within a polished story. When I told the African

American and Appalachian tale of "Taileybone" recently for seven hundred kids in West Virginia, I decided to play with the size of the monster. I said, "This creature was so big that it made Godzilla looked like a Muppet." I did not rehearse this thought, but because I was experienced with play, I had learned to let go, so in live performances I can word dance with my audience. This helped give new life to a story I have told for over fifteen years.

Environment for Word Dancing

Here are some tips to help create the most effective environment that invites word dancing. As much as you need to be in a state of readiness, you also have to find the most effective place to work so that you can be ready. It is difficult to work under the watchful eye of someone that is not connected to your work. It is hard to practice in a room where you have to whisper or have limited range with your body.

Find your comfort in telling. I practiced my stories walking around in my apartment for years. A little old man who always walked his tiny dog when he saw me talking to myself would rush to the other side of the road opposite from me. One time when he veered, I waved my hand for him to stop. I walked over to him and stood directly in front of him. I could see his knees shake as I spoke. I confided that I was a storyteller and would like for him to listen to my story. I told the story I was practicing. He did not say a word and rushed to the other side of the street. I hung my head and went back in my apartment. The next week I was practicing my stories and in no time he and his dog stood in front of me and said, "Do you have a story for us today?"

Story has the power to influence others and reduce fear. However, there are times when you need to have time to practice, not so others can hear the story, but so you can hear the story and imagine the work performed. You are the first audience. As tellers, even when we are telling for someone else, we are present. Our first audience is us. We are there for all stages of development, paying closer attention to ourselves as not only the teller of the story, but also the creator of the story.

Find a comfortable space. If you are in a hotel, check the walls and the sound. Find a place where you can explore the range of your voice and body movements—a place to play. Ideally, an empty room is effective, but you can word dance almost anywhere people can't hear you or don't mind. A park, room, and outdoors are all effective spaces. One must have the mindset of play. It is a wonder that even a hallway can be a perfect place to practice a story. Prepare to practice and play

Feel free to be the fool and the sage. The Japanese proverb, "We're fools whether we dance or not, so we might as well dance" reminds when we are practicing, we can't worry about how we look, sound, or act. We need to have the full range of experiences, even to dance badly. Don't practice in a place where you are intimidated or self-conscious. Instead, practice where you can be "naked"—in a metaphorical sense, the other sense might get you in trouble. Laugh in a way uncharacteristic of you and speak in various tones that make you comfortable as well as uncomfortable. Play with the choices you make with your voice and body. Basically dance with your words so you can feel the pattern, rhythm, and activity. We need to recognize the drama inherently in all story-crafting. First, story-crafters need to realize that all stories have dramatic dimensions.

I recently shared oral exercises with a well-known storyteller. She quickly dismissed the work, calling it "drama." She said this as though drama was separate from the work of story-crafting. The Irish writer and playwright Oscar Wilde said of drama, "I regard the theatre as the greatest of all art forms, the most immediate way in which a human being can share with another the sense of what it is to be a human being." The irony is that this storyteller is dramatic when she performs. Why as story-crafters do we separate the arts? In order to prepare to word dance, one must recognize that all art forms can help build our dance. Although we don't intend to act on stage in a rehearsed theatrical role, we can still use dramatic elements to explore how to better explain and tell the human story. We often connote using drama as expelling talent to a stage with a company of actors. Drama is more than that. It explores who we are by studying and sharing it louder and stronger, often for a listening audience. However, there is an internal as well as external drama that shows us quietly the value of a soft whisper, a hushed silence, and an awkward pause. As story-crafters, drama is an additional tool for us to help explore our full potential. This is why we need to allow ourselves to be serious and foolish. Have fun with it, but also realize there will be sage moments when you need to reflect. Let the work show the brilliance that resides in your choices. Use the full range of drama to help shape your stories.

I recently created a story where I take the legendary Jack, the same one who climbed the beanstalk, and compare his story with my own. You can see this at http://www.youtube.com/watch?v=Be1eFV3Cq94. The story uses caves as a metaphor to describe my journey from being a boy to becoming a man. My late Uncle Homer had once shared with me that there are secret caves that reside in Clay County, West Virginia. This was the place I used to vacation every year growing u It is where my mother was raised. There were details about those caves that did not make it into the story. They would be considered sketchy to talk about and probably would not make it in the story. However, in using play, I did not censor where I wanted to explore. I just needed to explore everything that was said in developing the story. I needed to re-experience the story. In doing so, I remembered something that my Uncle said, "All we have in this world son, is our name. Stay true to your family name. This is part of our honor." By playing with these dramatic times, I was able to use this later.

Practice with intention—work with significance. Russian dance choreographer and dancer Mikhail Baryshnikov said, "I do not try to dance better than anyone else. I only try to dance better than myself." Don't be idle in your practice time. Designate a time to practice. If you are tired, lazy, bored, you bring that energy to your word dancing. You can lift yourself out of it, but you have to work harder to do so. If you are not ready to play, practice mindfulness and breathing. Remember, breathing helps you to transfer out of the real time and into playtime. Dorothy Heathcote said when giving advice to young teachers that they should teach "with significance" (1984). We need to make the time we work significant and sometimes to find this, we need to let go to find it. We need to be restless to find what is meaningful in our work. She states,

> We need, too, to allow ourselves to be restless spirits—to be in the process of becoming.... I'm talking about the spirit that says, 'I can see where they're at'... It's the restlessness that, while confirming what is understood, leads on to the next mystery. (23)

Work with a sense of determination and understanding that your work is authentic and meaningful. Let your word dancing and play mean something. Position your work in play to be as important as the written work or performance.

Reflect, write down observations—keep a word dancing journal. It helps to have language that helps us remember ideas because we describe them well. Keep a reflection journal. This is not a word-for-word account, but instead words that bring back the story or a significant time in the story.

What is a Word Dancing Journal?

A word dancing journal records what you have learned from these exercises. It is not a place to write down a full story, but instead create trigger words or scenes to recapture your experiences and thoughts. You can jot as much or as little as you want. A word- dancing journal is an essential reflection tool.

These are notes that invite you to remember what you discover during your verbal word dancing. Sketch out significant moments and create visual pictures to help you remember the scenes. Dr. Rives Collins, co-author of *The Power of Story: Teaching Through Storytelling* (1997), invites "characteristic language" to recall story. Language is critical to the story. For "Little Red Riding Hood," one must have the words, such as, "My, what a big mouth you have …" This is worth writing down to remember and recall later. This is evocative of the story. A word dancing journal can be a place to list ideas and specific words.

You can also remember story by drawing. Instead of simply drawing stick figures, take time to draw the details of the story. Use a mini storyboard, which contains handwritten boxes, similar to a comic strip, to detail the action. Draw with intention. Be specific. I could easily draw a cave from the Jack story but this cave had specific markings. The more details I add, the more I remember the story.

This book consists of many activities that can be enhanced by jotting down reflections after each activity. Here are some general questions that you can use to help you remember any of the activities in the book.

1. What new language did you find from this experience? We can recall experiences from echoing the language used during the activity. Echoing is a practice of writing down what was said and thinking over the language.

2. If I had to describe my playful experience, what high detail

words would I use to recall the experience? High detail words are words are visible words to help you envision, and in turn reflect on the activity.

3. Did anything make me pause? Pausing is a sure detection that something significant happened. Jot down pauses so you can use and remember them later.

4. Are there any patterns that you experienced or noticed? Patterns also highlight a significant moment in your play.

5. What is the rhythm of your playful experience? Jotting a few words about the rhythm of the story can help you make decisions about tone, rate, and even impact of your playful experience.

It is also useful to write a paragraph about your experience. Although it is short, make it detailed. You will be surprised what you notice. Each exercise is engineered to help you with a specific focus. Write down what you discovered about the experience. Note: The premise is not to write down everything that happened. You need to word dance or talk it out before you write it out.

Rationale for the Exercises

At Kent State University, Professor Lucinda Holshue introduced to me Uta Hagan's exercises and text, *Respect for Acting* (1973). Hagen explains the how and why behind the work of the actor. I learned to value both conducting exercises that are meaningful and significant and how to explore in-depth exploration of character, scene, and relationship Hagan states, "When the activities state pieces of business, you are using them wrong" (2002, DVD). Exercises can help story-crafters develop ideas. As the adage says, "show don't tell," but with these exercises, one can do more than show. The story-crafter can experience what he or she is thinking and it is revealed in the exercise. Borrowing from Hagan's essential questions, I have created questions to elevate the work of our craft in story. They are applicable for storytellers, writers, and other imaginative thinkers.

Start with an Idea

An idea is prime material for play. For the last two years, I have been examining the problem of bullying behavior in the schools. My students and I have created an anti-bullying website at www.ourstoriescount.com. The site chronicles how we address anti-bullying behaviors through narratives, both fictional and real. I was wondering, what if I address bullying using the fairytale of "Little Red Riding Hood?" As I drifted off to sleep, I wondered, what if the wolf was a bully and Red was aware of bully prevention? In order to guide me in my future play with the idea, I began to talk out loud with the following:

> Red was her name. People say it was because she always wore that crimson cloak that her grandmother gave her, but it could also be because of the color of her cheeks when she talked to strangers. Red was shy, at least with people she didn't recognize.

With these story ideas to guide me, I began to word dance with this idea. In many of the exercises listed in this chapter, I will use this idea as a model to demonstrate my word dancing. As you read, you will see how this story takes on new directions and ideas. First, begin with an idea and then seek out the environment to word dance.

Exercise One: Questions to Address when Practicing Alone

This series of exercises address important questions for story-crafters. They are intended to extend story-crafters' range with the story. They are to be practiced out loud. Please note that although I had a set of questions to work, I did stray from them. It is natural to veer, change, or even neglect the questions in appreciation of another direction. After my own play practice, I found that the questions did change. However, the initial questions were effective building blocks with which to orchestrate my playful work.

Below is a list of questions for you to play with in order to improve your story crafting skills. They are playful practices that will assist in the development of the story you are crafting. Take some time with these questions and allow your ability to grow from the playful exercises.

This powerful first exercise can help create possible directions for story development.

1. What are the voices that are heard or not heard in the story?
2. What time is it?—Century, year, season, day, minute
3. What *troubles* are in the story?
4. What does the environment look like?
5. What does the environment, which we don't see, look like?

6. What are the obstacles that affect reactions?—Past, present, and future events.
7. How do the characters relate to each other? How do you know?
8. What does the main character want? What does that character want to avoid?
9. What is in the main character's way?
10. What does the character do to get what he or she wants? Is this new or do is there a past history of this?

Purpose of the exercise—Framing the story, these exercises will help you create building blocks for your narrative. The questions do not need to be followed chronologically. Work with the questions that move you closer to the story. For each of the questions, simply talk out loud to address and/or answer the question. However, detail your answer. Explore other responses to drift into new awareness. If the responses transform into scenes, let them. Relax. Allow your imaginative thinking to take action. You will be surprised at the result.

Discuss out loud—For each of the questions, say the question out loud. Think of what the question is asking and then reflect on it.

Talk out the response—Talking ideas out loud allows you to envision what you are crafting. There is a shape to sound. The sound of the voices carries an image. The words we use and vocally speak create pictures. We should use this tool to help us shape the story we are making.

In this chapter I provide a working model. I use the Little Red anti-bullying idea that I mentioned before. Instead of writing the ideas down for this chapter, I talked them out loud first while recording myself, then wrote down what I said for this chapter using the actual transcription of my oral conversation.

1. *What are the voices that are heard or not heard in the story?* What is meant here is: "who are the people that are speaking or active in your story?" Talking out loud about these people helps you to know them. However, there are also people with smaller roles who are only mentioned. These people might be discussed and used in your story play. Talking out loud helps you know the importance of these people. These can all be vital voices for play.

Example from transcription:
We know we have a wolf, the grandmother, and we have Red, but I have added new dimensions when thinking of telling the story. We now have a guidance counselor who works at the school, but he is relatively new. Red might have a little brother who has been picked on by other students. Red has watched this. The little brother might have special needs. Red might go to the library and work with the librarian. Red's mother has just had a bitter divorce. Red's mother is working really hard to communicate with her daughter. It is harder to do so since she is almost a teenager. As a parent, especially a single parent …

2. *What time is it? (Century, year, season, day, minute)* First, discuss the time in which the story takes place. Time is more than chronological time. Instead, it refers to how you understand the place of the story. Is it set in modern times? If so, does this mean your character would wear something different? What language is evocative of that time? If it takes place during Shakespearean time, what would they have, or not have, to be representative of the time? Talking out loud about how time affects the story can affect the direction of the story.

Example from transcription:
I am thinking of the story. I am thinking it is more modern: it might occur in the year 2012. It might be 2012 because I am referring to a guidance counselor, and one thing moves another, but it could be in the 1950s, but something makes me think it is more modern. I want to stick with the fact that it is in the fall. The leaves are turning, winter is approaching, and it is definitely in the fall. I am also thinking about the senses of the story. In the woods, in the fall, you can hear the brittle leaves; it sets a tone for Little Red's journey.

3. *What troubles are in the story?* Instead of thinking what happens in the story or providing plot points that create the conflict, think of the various types of trouble for each character. How does the environment support or not support the trouble? How does the trouble change when in another character's hands? Does a new trouble emerge?

Example from transcription:
The one thing that I can decide from the play we have already done is that Red is shy. There might be a wolf that is a bully and

even threatens her but she is shy. This might be a story about overcoming that. Along those lines, the mother is reticent. She, in turn, is shy with her daughter. She makes attempts to reconcile with her after this divorce. But she is shy in a different way.

4. *What does the environment look like?* There is a physical landscape created from the story. Think and talk about this out loud. How does the environment affect the tone, mode, and actions of the characters? Talking out loud can help you envision the scenes. This oral play can help you picture the story as you say it.

   Example from transcription:
   Obviously we have Red's home; it is probably not a large mansion after the divorce. This makes me think, what did the father do or what does the mother do for a living? Is she a stay-at-home mother? Does she work two jobs? What is going to complicate that trouble? We have the school and I don't think it is a top-notch school but I don't think it is at the bottom either. Let us look at the woods. What can we see? Menacing woods in the fall, eerie sounds, maybe you can hear animals but you can feel the desolation that the woods can sometimes have.

5. *What does the environment, which we don't see, look like?* There is so much in the story that is hinted at or just suggested. Talk out loud about what this might look like. Paint the images of what you don't see. This can take you to places that might be used in the story or offer backstories. As it is stated, "the devil is in the details." The more detailed your play is, the more vivid the environments and the relationships around it are.

   Example from transcription: The father's house is in a one-room house. Is it far away in New York City and it is so far away you can't travel to it. Is he a writer? Nothing is in the refrigerator. How would this impact Little Red? We also can't see the basketball court at the school but Little Red might like to play basketball or she might like someone who plays basketball. Maybe the basketball court has two purposes—one that is the place she is bullied so she avoids it. But at the same time, it also the place she watches a certain boy play ball because she has a small crush on him. Plus, the basketball court is the place where she feels most comfortable. She enjoys playing basketball.

6. *What are the obstacles that affect reactions?—Past, present, and future events.* This does not require a plot summary, but instead talk out loud about how the story changes due to the obstacles placed in certain characters' ways. Look at how the interplay of these reactions creates more situations for the characters.

   Example from transcription:
   We know that Red is shy, but it might be the wolf that is the person who changes this. The wolf is such a bully that Red realizes that she can't be quiet in life. So the wolf causes her to change from being shy to acting brave.

7. *How do the characters relate to each other? How do you know?* Drawing on the interplay mentioned in the last question, think how many of these characters would get along with one another. Who would have coffee with whom? What would they do to avoid each other?

   Example from transcription:
   Does the grandmother really relate to the mother or have they not been talking since the divorce? Is the grandmother the one who comforts the mother? Could that be why Little Red needs to go to her grandmothers so the mother can share messages with her? Is Little Red the conduit? Although the guidance counselor is friendly, is Red so shy she doesn't really take any of the advice?

8. *What does the main character want? What does that character want to avoid?.* This requires you to play out loud with the deep needs of what the main character wants. How do you know this? What keeps her from getting to her goal? Ask yourself, "What is keeping the main character from moving forward? Is what is holding her back worth extending or reducing?"

   Example from transcription:
   Obviously the main character is Red and what she wants, deep down, is to be heard. She wants a voice. She wants no one to pick on her and she wants to have the strength to tell that people to leave her alone. She has an identity, but what does she want to avoid? She wants to avoid all of the things in life because she would rather sit on her bed and read a book, write, draw, paint, or whatever she finds as her escape. Maybe her escape is at her grandmother's. Maybe only her grandmother realizes she needs this time by herself.

9. *What's in the main character's way?* Dig deep into the obstacles that are in the way. Why does she want this? What is in the way? How does she deal with these obstacles? We need to physically talk out what is in the way. Obstacles can be seen or unseen. For example, the wolf could be angry because a human did something to him as a cub, such as keeping him in a cage. Because of this he does not see humans as friends. The obstacle can also be something seen such as a wall that separates the house from the woods. Talking these things out makes them visible.

Example from transcription:
The first thing you want to say is the wolf is in her way. I think Red is in the way. We need to convince Red to do something differently to break out of her shell. Maybe it is the confrontation with the wolf that is the last straw. This is the point when Red says, "Stop! I am not going to show you my grandmother's house. I am not going to take you there." Perhaps this is where she has her own voice for the first time.

10. *What does the character do to get what he or she wants? Is this new or is there a past history of this?* This can be revealed from a physical action of the character or through words, spoken—verbal—and not spoken—internal—from the dialogue of the character. Now that you have established the obstacles in the story, what do the characters do to remove them? Is this enough? How can they do more? Less? What will build more trouble—tension—for the story?

Word dancing journal
- After playing with voices, what new voices did you discover? What did they sound like? How important were these voices to the story you want to tell? Who had the strongest voice?
- What new ways did you use time? How specific did the time become? Explain.
- Was there any unexpected trouble? How did you increase and/or decrease it?
- Describe the physical environment when you played with this story.
- What surprised you from your examination of the environment. What you did not see?
- List the obstacles that you discovered and write a sentence or two about what made them obstacles.

- What character did not get along with the other? What characters wanted to be closer? Why? Explain.
- What do the main characters desire most of all? Explain.
- What keeps each main character from achieving their desire?
- How did you attempt to remove what was in the character's way?

Exercise Two: Explode the Moment—Fuse and Diffuse

Purpose of the exercise—This is a way to extend a specific situation in a story so as to heighten—*explode*, or reduce—*diffuse*, moments in the story. The story-crafter revisits a chosen dramatic event in the story. Explore exploding or diffusing specific moments.

Discuss out loud—Talk out the major events in the story. Decide on the one or two events that could benefit from verbal play. You can do this by exploding or diffusing the specific action. Exploding the moment tells the story, but extends so that it becomes larger than life. Diffusing the moment tells the story, but extends it so that the moment becomes less significant. This intentionally makes you play with the story's journey by creating and working with the events to fit the play.

Ways to explode the moment
1. Tell the story, but when you arrive at the moment to explore, extend it for at least five sentences. Make it larger with each sentence.
2. Tell the story, but when you arrive at the moment to explore, extend it by having another character add to it.
3. Tell the story, but when you arrive at the moment to explore, explode the reaction to the event. In fact, make the event the central focus.
4. Tell the story, but when you arrive at the moment to explore, explode the actual language of the story by improvising the adjectives to describe it.

Ways to diffuse the moment
1. Consider all the major characters in the story. Pick someone who is large and make him or her smaller. To do so, you might have to make someone else larger. Someone who is larger plays a more central role. Someone who is smaller plays a lesser role in the story.

2. Consider the environment of the story and diffuse it. Make it smaller. If it takes place in the city of Chicago, change it to happen in the smaller neighborhood outside of Chicago: change it to be a small room on the South Side.
3. Consider the biggest trouble in the story and change it so it is smaller. However, again, you might have to make it happen. Let it happen naturally. Don't force it. Play.
4. Consider the ending of the story. Change it so it is smaller and a new ending is established.

Word dancing journal
- How did you make it larger? What things do you want to keep from this experience? Why?
- How did diffusing the moment change the tone? Do you want to keep it? Why or why not?
- Can you extend it anymore? How?
- Reflect in a paragraph on the experience. Study the observations.

Exercise Three: If This is True, What Else Is?

Purpose of the exercise—This is an exercise to expand the truth not necessarily told in the story.

Discuss out loud—Talk out what is accepted as truth. List, don't retell the story.

Activity—After you list the truths, ask yourself, "If this is true, then what is else is true?" Think about what else should be accepted and also what is not accepted in the story.

Example from transcription:
What is true is that Little Red is shy. What else is true is that she is not doing well in school because she has a speech class and she can't really get up there and talk. People make fun of her, especially the boy in the second row. In the last seat, I think that is the bully. What is true is that the mother feels hurt. She has taken on a second job, but is not getting enough hours. They really don't have a family dinner table anymore because they just don't get together.

Word dancing journal
- Are there any other truths omitted?

- How can you extend this truth?
- If this is truth, then what is a lie? How do you know?
- Write and reflect in a paragraph. Study it later.

Exercise Four: Tell Time:

Purpose of the exercise—It is important when telling or writing a story to manipulate the way the story is told. One way to manipulate it is to adjust the time it takes to tell it. A stopwatch or time-keeping device is needed for this exercise.

Discuss out loud—This assignment requires you to do the following:

1. Talk the story out loud, but tell it in one sentence. Write down that sentence in your word dancing journal. Pay particular attention to the sentence and why you have chosen the words. Tell me about the choices.
2. Talk out the story, but tell it in one minute. Write down what you left out and why in your word dancing journal.
3. Talk out the story, but tell it in five minutes. Write down what you left out and why in your word dancing journal.

Word dancing journal
- What elements did you keep each time?
- Was there something that was in all of them?
- Explore this—is there anything that needs more in the story?

Exercise Five: Telling Around the Story

Purpose of the exercise—Children book writers sometimes create more than the children's story by applying what is called back matter or even front matter to the story. This is more of the story that is contained in extra pages, the cover, before the story, and even in the *backdrop* of the illustrations. In this exercise, we consciously work on not telling the story; instead think of what is happening during the story. The story exists within an environment that we might talk out loud and see through play.

Discuss out loud—Don't think the story directly, but instead think about what is going on while the story is occurring. What has already happened? What could possibly happen? What is in the backdrop? What is meant by backdrop is what is happening around the story. For example, what if the story is about a first date, but it takes place in the fifties? What could be going on around the story? Perhaps there is a malt shop nearby or people are planning to attend a sock ho By talking around the story, the story-crafter may find a way to use what they find in the story.

> *Word dancing journal*
> - Reflect on and write about your exploration of the backdrop of the story.
> - Did you become aware of things that were left out and why you should or should not keep them?

Exercise Six: Change Genres—Diary, Letter, and Monologue

Purpose of the exercise—Story-crafters often only frame their work in story to write or tell. This requires the story-crafter to change the way the story is presented. As my friend and colleague, Robin Holland, author of *Deeper Writing* (2013), says, we can examine the work in a new container. This is achieved by switching the genre. This is the vessel that holds the story. A story might be contained and revealed in a letter or monologue. Each container or frame can help stories to be told and experienced differently.

Talk out loud—This exercise requires you to see this story, not in its present form, but in a new genre such as a letter, diary, or monologue. Play with the different frames and reflect on the results.

> *Example from transcription:*
> Dear father, I know we have not spoken for years, but I need to tell you what happened to me. I was in the woods. The same place you told me to not to go. But you are not around to tell me that anymore. It was dark. I needed to get medicine that grandma had for Billy. You remember Billy. He is your son. Billy is the person who calls out your name but you are not there. He is my brother. I have to explain to him why you are missing from our home. Anyway, I was in the woods …

> *Word dancing journal*
> - Reflect on how the use of different genres changed the story.
> - Did retelling through a different genre reveal or disguise a part of the story in a way that you can use?

Exercise Seven: Staying with Significance

Purpose of the exercise—Noted storyteller and coach Doug Lipman believes that we must know the *MIT* or *most important thing* (1999) in the narrative. This exercise helps recognize not only how to identify the MIT, but why it is significant.

Discuss out loud—

1. Talk out the MIT and address the questions:
2. Why is this the MIT?
3. What builds up the MIT?
4. What is fighting against the MIT?
5. What would be the secondary MIT if this were not present?

Word dancing journal
- Reflect on how you know the action that you have chosen is the most significant one?
- Explain why the MIT is important.

Exercise Eight: Backward and Forward Telling

Purpose of the Exercise—A story can start from anywhere. As Edmiston (2009) said to me once, "The best stories happen in the middle." Sometimes when you look at a story from other than the beginning or end, you find new ways to proceed with story.

Talk out loud—Tell the story by starting in the middle. Then, tell the story from the ending back to the beginning.

Word dancing journal
- Reflect on how this experience was new for you.
- Explain how backward and/or forward telling helped you to become aware of a new way to tell the story.

Exercise Nine: Telling with the Body—Silence Before Sound

Purpose of the Exercise— This exercise demonstrates how important the body is in conveying story. The body communicates a message. Most communication research suggests that we listen to a story nonverbally more we do verbally. What is known is that we see the story as it is being told through body language. This exercise uses play to see how the body might reveal your story.

Talk out loud—Not really. This is actually where you only mouth silently or think of the story while paying attention to how your body language creates it. Over seventy percent of meaning in communication is nonverbal.

1. Tell the story silently. Only mouth the words while allowing your body to clearly express what you are saying.
2. Don't mouth the words at all. Instead, try to have your body show certain significant times in the story. How would you create a physical picture of your story with your body? For example, if someone collapses in the story, then collapse. A collapse from a bullet is different than collapsing from exhaustion. Examine how this feels. Reflect on what this feels like and how you might add it or why you might not add it to your story.

Word dancing journal
- Draw each moment of significance.
- Include as much detail as you can.
- Reflect on how this exercise helped with your body awareness.

Exercise Ten: Let the Objects of the Story Tell the Story

Purpose of the story—This exercise helps the story-crafter to move away from sequential telling. In order to play with a new way of the telling the story, the objects in the story become central points in telling it. Pick three or four objects and tell the story from object to object. For example, in little Red's story, the basket of goodies is a central object. Instead of saying, "There was a little girl and her name was Red," you might start by making the basket central. Thus the narration might be something like, "Red come here, I have this basket I want you to deliver. It contains an apple, some medicine, and some homemade napkins I made. They are red, just like your favorite color." But don't stop here. Keep the objects in the story the subject of the telling. "My first basket was given to me by your grandmother. I used to carry it like you do now but ..."

Talk out loud—Tell from objects; make them significant and full of detail. Make your major transitions when you are switching from one object to another.

Word dancing journal
- Reflect on how this changed the way you see the story.
- Explain how the senses were involved in the description of the objects.

- What effect did this exercise have on the story development?

Exercise Eleven: Tell from Letters of the Alphabet—See How Far You Can Go

Purpose of the exercise—Another way to veer away from the order of the story is to force yourself to tell it in a within a new frame. For this exercise, you use all the letters in the alphabet. Each end word is a letter in the alphabet. Tell the story with each end word beginning with a letter of the alphabet.

> *For example*:
> The boy went to get an apple—the end word is A
> He did not like the apple, so he bought a brownie—the end word is B
> He was surprised when he saw it was not a brownie, but an apple flavored cookie—the end word is C

Talk out loud—Tell the story with each end word following the letters of the alphabet. Start with A and work your way down. However, try to add detail in each sentence. Don't over think it. Remember, this is play.

> *For example:*
> She stood on the wooden train with her red cloak, alone.
> She walked in trepidation but she walked boldly.
> She was reluctant to begin this journey to grandmother's cottage.
> She was shy, not daring.
> She had had enough.
> Bullying that was; it make her feel like a failure.

Word dancing journal
- How did the story remain the same during the exercise?
- How did the story become different?
- Reflect on changes to the story that you might make following this exercise.

Exercise Twelve: A Possible Ending

Purpose of the Exercise—Although you may not feel ready to end the story, you can always try alternative endings. Examine them and then choose what you want to keep and disregard.

For example:

Red stood alone, tightening her cape not because she was afraid, but because for the first time, she noticed she was cold. She was freezing. She wrapped her cape around her, but not to protect herself, just to keep herself warm. It had been a long time, but she sat and smiled, longing for hot chocolate.

Word dancing journal

- List different endings you explored and reflect on how they might change the story.
- Did you play with something in each ending that you might use? Make a list of these things.

Conclusion

Words can dance, but they have a hard time doing so when we write them down first. I hope the exercises in this chapter will help you to lift your story in new directions.

In the next chapter, we will explore how the hidden, and not so hidden, troubles or tensions in the story can help improve the playful story practice. We will share how stories are not developed by plot points, but instead by conflict and the relationships between and amongst the points of conflict. We will look at conscious and unconscious conflict. We will see what troubles the story. We will examine what trouble looks like and how working with it creates investment in the story direction. The next chapter will prepare you to use tension to move story in ways that are unexplored, unexplained, and unfinished.

Chapter 4
The Invisible Craft of Building a Story

How often does a storyteller reveal what is involved in making their stories work? They spellbind us by sharing vivid accounts that take us out of a chair and into the world of their narrative. With only their bodies and voices, they transport us to a fictional world, but how often do we see the behind-the -scenes work of the storyteller? Understanding of the storyteller's craft is most often invisible to audiences.

I was reminded of this invisibility when I hired my good friend and colleague Odds Bodkin—you can learn more about him at www.oddsbodkin. com—to perform the *Iliad* at Ohio Dominican University, where I teach storytelling. When he performed, time shifted as his voice and manner transformed to bring Homer's classic to our eyes and ears. His jawline changed to show the anger of the gods and just as quickly, altered to reveal the soft feminine voice of Agamemnon's mother. Speaking with expert design, precision and polish, the *Iliad* was alive in our auditorium.

With appreciation, I asked if he would consider sharing a second show. His response was swift, "Do you know what it took to build the first show?" Although I was used to performing many shows in one day, I had not been telling the *Iliad*. Bodkin detailed the work involved in creating the piece, explaining that a second show would demand different energy and rehearsal. Although I was a performer, for a moment, I had forgotten that each show requires different positioning, homework, practice and performance.

To reach Odysseus' baritone, Bodkin practices a series of vocal exercises. He prepares his guitar and vocal instrument at least an hour before each performance. To echo the tension of the story, he practices and plays with many choices. There is much invisible work, unseen to the listener. The performer's job is to make his or her craft seem effortless, but the craft of storytelling and story-making is far from this.

Storytellers share their finished performances. Although story-crafters, storytellers, and writers may craft many drafts and conduct vocal practices, the public and more often, other story-crafters, never witness it. Storytelling looks easy. The endless drafts and numerous practices remain unseen.

This invisibility creates a false impression of the work requirements needed to create the art. Too often people believe accomplished storytelling professionals like Jay O'Callahan, Elizabeth Ellis, or Donald Davis avoid practicing because they are so good or they have performed so often they have reached a threshold that renders practice unnecessary. The work of an accomplished—or beginning—teller is never over. Each teller prepares in his or her way. In his performances, Jay O'Callahan orchestrates his art. Although he does not memorize his work, he knows the rhythm of each performance. He does the homework necessary to be within that rhythm, creating a state of readiness. He centers his breathing and situates himself within the story.

All three tellers share the craft involved in their work and host coaching or intensives to share their crafting-making skills with others. Donald Davis travels the country, not only sharing his performance, but explaining his craft and the work involved in creating stories. He has recorded some of this on the DVD, *What's Your Story?* (2012), and chronicles it in the books such as *Telling Your Own Stories* (1993) and *Writing as a Second Language.* (2000). Elizabeth Ellis shares her tales, her personal stories in her latest book, *Every Day A Holiday* (2014), but also outlines her process of creating story in her work, *From Plot to Narrative* (2012). We can learn much from these storytelling experts by studying their models and discussing our work with other story-crafters.

The Work of the Story-Crafter

Picture the work of a story-crafter as a map that reveals new roads to the creation of new experiences. These roads direct anyone who follows the paths offered. Each road, tale, performance, and/or preparation affords the story-crafter to find new directions. In over twenty-eight years of sharing stories and workshops about the process, each show or workshop still leaves me with new awareness.

My experience performing for animators in Singapore demonstrated how to tailor a storytelling program so that this audience could learn about how crafting stories can help produce detailed images in computer-based design. In order to know more about how to market this program, I needed to deeply listen to the needs of this audience. Deep listening is more than hearing. It is focusing on what the audience needs. In order to talk about our craft, we need to have effective listening skills.

In my work with the Office of Special Events in Pigeon Forge, Tennessee, I needed to focus on listening to stories of American heroes and heroines, especially the stories of veterans. From this deep listening to veterans and other tellers who have researched American tales, I was able to create a nationwide program at local, regional, and national levels, honoring these stories and highlighting veterans' stories. The late, accomplished teller and two-time Vietnam vet Pat Mendoza listened to my plans. He became a sounding board for my ideas. He became rich counsel for the ideas. Pat's past work helped me with my ideas—he deeply focused on listening to all of them. He offered assistance only to support the cause.

This same mindset allowed me to serve as the Executive Director for the National Youth Storytelling Olympics—now Showcase. I needed to be a deep listener to make this work in the same way Pat listened to and helped me. I could not tackle these honors alone. I had to deeply focus on needs at all levels. The important criterion for deep listening is to open up story spaces where the listening can occur.

As story-crafters, our work expands richly when developing listening skills. A noted storyteller once said to me, "Kevin, I tell about one hundred stories, but I listen to thousands more. This is what makes me a good storyteller." As story-crafters, we need to seek out other crafters who will listen to our stories and our ideas for story programming. We need to open spaces for story ideas to be shared so that a collaborative understanding of our art grows. When I was with the late, great Jackie Torrence, she was troubled by storytellers who count the number of stories they could tell to others. She said some list their stories like they are catalogues. I will never forget when she said, she was not concerned with the number of stories someone knows, but rather with "Does the teller have the right story for the person right now?" We need to consider this as we focus our listening skills. We need to value the deep listening that occurs when we are focused on the cause. If that cause is story-crafting for someone else, we need to value this as our direction.

Opening Story Spaces

Once story spaces open in your community, people notice. In California, I lived near the Tachi-Yokut tribe. One of the members of the tribal council discovered that I had created story spaces for students in the form of a club and/or troupe at the high school where I taught. The council then asked if I would come and share stories with their elders. During the months we were allowed, my students and I had the rich honor of telling stories biweekly. We were able to create more story spaces; to build a community of stories.

Adapting Story-Crafting

In storytelling, one method will not work in all situations. In fact, storytelling audiences can be found in all fields. Dr. Richard Stone in his book: *The Healing Art of Storytelling: A Sacred Journey of Personal Discovery* (1996) insists that his nurses and all health care hospital attendants know their patients' stories before addressing their symptoms. In *Narrative Inquiry: Experience and Story in Qualitative Research* (Clandinin and Connelly 2000), teachers are studying their own stories to discover what teaching means. Big hotel chains have hired storytellers to help advertise their hotel's story. Each field creates new direction for story-crafters. Books like *The Storytelling Animal* (Gottschall 2012) demonstrate how stories are inherent in our thinking process and why scientists are giving more consideration to storytellers. Accomplished educator and storyteller Kendall Haven, author of *Story Proof: The Science Behind the Startling Power of Story* (2007) has been hired by NASA to map the storytelling brain. As Haven states on his website, story is a natural way to make meaning.

> Combining research from 16 fields of science, Haven uncovered the first-ever scientific proof that story structure is evolutionarily hardwired into human brains. From birth, humans automatically make sense, understand, comprehend,

and remember through stories. Story is how we humans *think!* (Havens n.d.)

Storytelling is used in many fields. The book, *Whoever Tells the Best Story Wins* (Annette Simmons, 2007) successfully promotes story use in business. However, in all story-crafting arenas, each place issues its own demands and audiences. It is a craft that we need to improve upon, based on the demands or the type of story work we do and for whom we do it. Play helps storytellers adapt to all these needs and audiences. Adopting a mindset that invites continual practice and play with each performance creates a better understanding of the craft.

Mindset

Tellers cannot afford to listen to those who encourage them not to practice. Instead they need to listen and prepare themselves for each performance; to respect and improve in their art. Deep listening is vital to a story-crafter's work. This skill takes practice. I was reminded of this when professional storyteller and author Dan Keding left a storytelling tent, turned around and shared something that I try to never forget. He explained that the reason he stepped out was because he had performed all day and could not concentrate on the teller with the full listening strength needed. He returned later when he had better energy with which to listen.

Talking About our Craft

We not only need to listen to other story-crafters, but we need to vocalize about our work. In order to reveal the invisible process of story-crafting, we need to share promises, unexpected discoveries, mistakes and celebrations. We need to voice the process of discovery and not be reluctant to use play to explore deeply. When visible, story-crafting creates authentic learning for beginners and it honors the work of experienced tellers. We need to study advanced story-crafters' offerings.

Expanding our Work

Too often storytellers and story listeners arrange gatherings only to tell stories, but storytelling is a craft that needs to be vocalized and shared. We need to make time to share our work with each other. I am reminded when Dan Yashinsky, a prominent Canadian storyteller, says that storytellers need to know two things: how to move furniture and make tea. In a real sense we need to make space to sit down and talk about our craft. We need not be in a rush. As much as time is designated to create a tea ceremony, we need to sit and sip in the learning that comes when we share with each other. Story-crafters need to talk about how their stories were formed and why—not during a performance, but at times that are designated as a time to meet with storytellers and story designers. They also need to be open to how dancers, rap artists, story-slammers, traditional and nontraditional writers, and visual and performing artists work. Story-crafters need to recognize, realize, and accept the media, artists, businesses and teachers that use story. We are not alone in our work. Shared participation and exploration create spaces for storytelling and writing guilds to encourage discussions of the process, instead of concentrating on the final story as the product and end goal of their meetings. Feedback at all stages of story development, from the first idea to the last sentence, creates a community that supports our development and uses play to engage in our choices.

Building Communities of Collaboration

We are creating an invisible community with other story-crafters, writers, storytellers, guild members, and even promising future storytellers, both youth and adults. How can we be imaginative thinkers if we hide how we conduct our art?

Using Play to Make Stories Visible

Engaging in the art of story-crafting is an effective way to share the process. There is no better engagement than play because it reveals the invisible work of creating story, making the invisible visible. Although play has its own expectations and rules, it invites more freedom to explore and make choices. Working with "Little Red Riding Hood", we must stay in the fiction to be able to play in the world where Red lives. These are the rules of the fiction—unless you deliberately want to place Red in outer space and in play, this can be done. If rules exist in the fiction, how do we increase the investment in the play while paying attention to the rules? How do we focus on the story, not simply as retelling plot, but instead diving in deep engagement with the fiction? Story-crafters can find or create trouble in their work to deepen engagement.

What is Trouble?

Children are told to avoid trouble and to, "not to get in trouble when going out." Behaving like proper adults means keeping away from trouble. Storytellers often tell stories about trouble. Brer Rabbit, Anansi, and Coyote are examples of tricksters who are often are in trouble—or they seek it out. There is an old folktale about an alligator that confronts trouble in the form of a large fire. The alligator's friends remind him, "Don't trouble trouble until trouble troubles you." But the alligator does not listen and instead taunts trouble. Thus, the flaming trouble consumes the alligator. The message is twofold: don't look for trouble, because it will find you; when it does, leave it alone. Trouble can harm and often does, when discovered. However, writers, storytellers, and other imaginative thinkers view trouble as the necessary ingredient to make a story work. Story-based trouble is something not to be avoided, but rather to seek, because it improves the story development. Unresolved trouble can be intentionally developed to increase the story's movement.

For example, in the story *Peter Pan*, Captain Hook brings trouble. However, using playful exercises outlined in this chapter, one can explore what is inherent in Captain Hook that makes him create the trouble for Peter. Outside of his ordeal with the alligator, there might be other reasons that Peter is the target of his wrath. One can playfully explore with other events in Hook's life. Perhaps explore a time when he was a child and his father yelled at him and called him worthless, or even talk out loud about how he feels about Peter. Each exercise asks the story-crafter to use his or her imaginative thinking to dig deep into the character or find the reason for the trouble.

Story-Based Trouble

Exploring the trouble within story helps the story-crafter experience the work differently. Perhaps there is another dimension of Peter Pan that makes him work extra hard to remain a child. Using play to explore this direction can make this real. Imaginative thinking is active and can affect a character, relationship, dialogue, demand, or other details in a working story. A working story is one that has not been finalized. When trouble acts as a verb, it agitates the ordinary to disrupt, creating more directions. Conflict moves story. As noted, social psychologist Jerome Bruner said, "Trouble is the engine of narrative" (1996 99).

Imagine concentrating on the story's conflict. Step outside of the story to examine what happened before or after the story. Are issues yet to be explained or are they unresolved? Do characters still need to be fleshed out? Do they display hidden trouble? Trouble may be found in the external environment. In the novel, *The Hobbit* by J. R. R. Tolkien, Bilbo encounters the dragon Smaug and his lair. In the description of the lair, we witness the many battles that occurred with Smaug. Broken shields and swords, lost treasures, and artifacts of visitors who did not survive are all part of the description. By playing with creating and envisioning one of these stories, we might reveal why the dragon is so distrustful of humans and Halflings. In play, this is possible.

Although trouble is the engine of story, in traditional story-crafting circles, it is not. Most story-crafters work from plot chronologically. Instead of concentrating on *what* happened, let us examine *why* something happened. Trouble brings the story-crafter closer to why. How did this character get to be so mean? Who made him this way? Why did he not fight becoming mean? How did he develop as a mean villain? Did it occur over time or all at once? Story-crafters, do more than consciously ask, "What is the trouble of the story?" Rather, extend your questions to address how the characters, environment, and dialogue are driven by trouble. We need to place the emphasis of our story-crafting on trouble, not just the order of events.

What is Wrong with Chronological Organization?

In the play stage of story-crafting, order is not as important. Engaging in play will create a natural order. Concentrating sequentially on a story only helps one build an outline. Story-crafters may miss out on the invisible part or the behind-the-scenes fictional work that forms the story. What happens before and after a given scene can make for an effective playful experience. Exploring those happenings can help create a deeper investment for teller and listener in the scene or idea. For example, if you are only working on the plot, one can't pause or examine more closely a specific story event. Take for example the story of King Arthur. Pausing to explore the first time King Arthur meets Guinevere, can deepen the first love feeling of this famous couple. You could concentrate on this special moment by highlighting the senses that might occur during this time. How did she smell when Arthur reached for her hand? How did he smell? What was the scent of the day or the ground? Unless time is provided to work and expand on these areas in the story, they are invisible. The story crafter must pause the story to develop it more. But if we work simply on a plot, we do not develop these needed areas for the story. This is the behind-the-scenes work that makes the story flow. If your story sequence is based on plot, understanding plot is the result. It is not enough to say, "Then Little Red reaches grandmother's house." However, if you use play to organize possible story ideas or directions, you can pause to explore how Red arrives at grandmother's house. What did the woods look like? Perhaps even pause the story to concentrate on the sound of her breathing. These are hidden times that are within the skeleton of the story, but not yet fleshed out. For example, focusing exclusively on the wolf's arrival at grandmother's house, you might miss Red's encounter with a mystery wildflower, and as told by her grandmother, with powers to put someone to sleep. This extends or even changes the story, and in play, it is permitted. Happy accidents abound in story crafting.

Happy Accidents when Talking Out Loud

Through play, story-crafters can discover a happy accident, which is something new in the story or story development. Happy accidents cannot develop without hearing a story told out loud. With "Little Red Riding Hood", the wolf still waits for Red whether she stops for flowers or not. In play, we are inside of the story, seeing it as it unfolds. Storytellers might discover new adventures and story lines each time they speak it out loud. As Pat Schneider (2003) states, "talking is just writing in the air." It can become more than this because talking invites the story-crafter to envision or experience the story differently than when writing. They can play with the character's voice, choosing the right word or sound to create the eerie woods, or even to create a dramatic effect when the character falls off the cliff. Talking out loud is the closest you will come to hearing, and consequently experiencing, the story as it is being developed. While writers develop the internal voice, story-crafters play out loud practicing and hearing the delivery, which is not possible when writing. For example, as Red walks into the darkness, the story-crafter can share out loud how the sky darkens ominously, warning Red to go home. Even if Red continues to grandmother's house, the happy accident foreshadows what is ahead.

Exploring Trouble Spots in a Story

Introducing play explores unresolved trouble spots. There can also be potential trouble spots, where tension or possible tension can be intensified to improve the story-crafting experience. This trouble here is called story-based trouble. Trouble arises from needs or wants. "I want to save this man from a fire." "I want to be rich." "He wants this person to be quiet." This trouble is about wanting or needing something, whether it is resolved it or not, the want is there. The intensity of the want can build the degree of tension. As Kurt Vonnegut shares in the *Paris Review*, this want is vital to all stories.

> When I used to teach creative writing, I would tell the students to make their characters want something right away—even if it's only a glass of water. Characters paralyzed by the meaninglessness of modern life still have to drink water from time to time. One of my students wrote a story about a nun who got a piece of dental floss stuck between her lower left molars, and who couldn't get it out all day long. I thought that was wonderful. The story dealt with issues a lot more important than dental floss, but what kept readers going was anxiety about when the dental floss would finally be removed. Nobody could read that story without fishing around in his mouth with a finger. (1977)

What is Story-Based Trouble?

Story-based trouble describes the degree of tension created from either telling or crafting story. To understand how to use trouble or tension, story must be examined in parts. Stories are comprised of many episodic scenes with beats that set the pace and rhythm. As Will Dunne states in *The Dramatic Writer's Companion: Tools to Develop Characters, Cause Scenes, and Build Stories* (2009):

> Just as a full-length dramatic story is made up of acts, and each act is made up of scenes, each scene is made up of beats. Beats are simply the smallest units of dramatic action. They come in different sizes and have different functions, but most have a similar structure, which mirrors the structure of both the scene and the story. (170)

Stories are not simply comprised of plot statements. Instead, as Dorothy Heathcote reminds us in her comments about drama, it consists of episodes. An episode is made of a series of events that create the scene. Story has many complementary and competing scenes. When one scene works with another, trouble and possible trouble may arise, creating tension among the scenes. In the story of "Little Red Riding Hood", the quiet scene with Red's mother asking for a grandmother's visit is quite different than discovering a wolf in the bed. The later has greater tension and even more areas to play with possible tension. The physical tension can occur when Red searches for a place to run, or perhaps she decides to stay where she is. The story beats lead up to her decision. The story-crafter might decide to accelerate her fear, by subsequently increasing Red's stutter as she addresses the wolf. The beats intensify, her feet shift, her eyes search for an exit, and the wolf growls. Fear beats on with the desired result—a frightened Red.

Beats take the temperature of an episode. Story-crafters can manipulate story-making decisions and then act on them. They can examine if various beats are significant, and then decide to look for trouble. The wolf attack is hot but grandmother's memories of childhood might be cold. Hot and cold moments create visualized story beyond plot. Playing with the story allows the story-crafter to change the temperature or tension.

For example, the story abruptly transforms when the wolf arrives, creating a different beat. Red prances until the wolf descends, growling and extending his teeth. Maybe we can smell the wolf's pungent gritty odor in sharp contrast to Red's finely pressed hood. This changes the tone and has the potential to increase the temperature or tension; highlighting trouble within the story.

Drama and Tension

Drama activates tension. Spoken work creates a dramatic experience. A story-crafter is a skillful engineer of sound, body, and movement—all the tools of drama. A story-crafter voices an action, making it dramatic. When a story-crafter uses play to change vocal and body choices, the drama is accentuated. Drama explores the moments that elevate or decrease intensity in a scene or narrative. Heathcote (1994) believed dramatic tension is, "worthwhile tension" (34). Drama and story are interlinked. Each story-crafter is also a dramatist and this too is a worthwhile combination. As David Booth (2005) notes,

> Drama allows us to tell stories, to engage in the art of the
> narrative. The simplest retelling of yesterday's events is an

act of imagination, as we have the option of reinventing the characters, the experience, the circumstances, the motivations and the outcomes. (13)

As story-crafters, we need to recognize that we are narrative specialists who use drama to envision and enact our stories. Drama and story create rhythm.

Rhythm of the Story

Story has both an internal and external rhythm measured when playing with the beats. Story-crafters can create internal rhythm when a character thinks out loud and an external rhythm when a character avoids or creates tension. A charging wolf changes the rhythm, evoking a new beat. Some rhythmic beats may be underdeveloped. When the teller reduces or increases the tension, he or she will understand and see how the story rhythm is created.

However, don't get so tied up listening to the beats that you lose the story. Remember, playing with the beats accentuate the possibilities of story, but let the story be told. It is possible to play with the story too much so that you end up changing the entire direction. Be ready for change, but stay true to the narrative you want to share. Ask if the change is necessary. Don't change beats or temperature if it does not lead closer to the story.

Practice Exploration of Tension and Beats within the Story

In this chapter, several exercises explore the tension or trouble in the story. Before you engage in these exercises, practice with the example outlined below. It is useful to play with a non-personal story in order to concentrate on understanding the exercises. This will make sense later when you work with your own story ideas.

> *A specific episode in the story*—On the way to his father's kingdom, young Prince Aaron became lost. He discovered a shiny coin in a fountain, but he remembered his father said he must not stop for any reason. Instead, he must arrive home before night falls. The coin grew brighter and brighter with each step as his will power decreased.

> *To consider*—Examine the story. Uncover the trouble and possible trouble spots. Consider how you might increase the temperature. Think out

loud as you ponder the questions. Ask yourself the following questions:

1. **What is the trouble of the story?**

   Thinking out loud—When talking out loud, I notice the first trouble is that he is lost. Imagine what that means? In what way is he lost? How did he become lost? Why is his father worried about him being lost? Did something happen on previous travels that made the king worry? Perhaps explore the metaphor of lost as it relates to who he is and how he cares or does not care about his travels.

   Look for possible trouble areas and explain how they might enhance the story—A possible trouble area is his lack of will power as the coin becomes unusually bright. What are the possibilities or directions that can come from this event? Another possible trouble area is the time of the day. Perhaps the woods become darker and darker and he cannot find his way. This way we wonder if he will ever find his way out of the woods.

2. **What are the tensions of the characters?**

   Thinking out loud—In this case the boy brings tension to himself. The way he sees himself in this journey can affect the outcome of his travels. However, the father is also traveling with him. He is constantly reminded of his father's order. His father is also the King so this intensifies his power over his son. This can be true, unless his son is a rebel and does not listen to his father. His father has a strong influence on his choices. How can you play with these ideas to bring more tension?

3. **What are the tensions or trouble spots caused by the environment?**

   Thinking out loud—In orally discussing the environment, I realize that the woods create an image as I tell the story. Here might be a place for the senses to play a part in your thinking out loud. What are the sounds of the woods? Do they calm or disturb Prince Aaron? What is the feel of the woods? Do trees populate the area? What are the noises, animals and landscape like? Are the trees dead in the middle of winter or do they show life as spring is on the rise? Is the air warm or cold? What does it smell like? Work with the senses help to complicate the story?

4. **Does the dialogue invite trouble?**

   Thinking out loud—The dialogue here is internal, what else might the boy be thinking? Why is he thinking this and how will it affect his future steps? What was he thinking about right before this episode in the story? Does he miss someone he left back in the kingdom? Would this strengthen the need to return more quickly? Where is his mother? Does he have sisters? A girlfriend? Lover? How did they meet? Why does he let the relationship continue despite his father's power over him? Remember, "how" and "why" are the biggest questions to ask when playing with story.

Exploring the Beats of the Story

In order to alter the story, examine the beats as possible places to change tension or trouble. For example, when Aaron sees the coin, what is he thinking about? Perhaps on his last journey, there was a time when his father yelled at him for making a mistake. He might be remembering how he could not leave the castle for two weeks because he lost the letter he was supposed to deliver. This would change his inner dialogue. In what way can you increase the number of beats leading up to his decision to take the coin?

Looking closely at the story, we notice that suddenly, Prince Aaron realizes that he is alone in the woods, in the dark. Play with the environment to create even more possible trouble. See this episode as it occurs in escalating beats—it gradually becomes dark, he begins to worry, and the light on the fountain is the only light, and he wants the coin. At last, there is a release of tension when he grabs the coin, despite his father's commands.

Reflection Questions

Now examine a different story using the same questions we used in the preceding example. Play with the trouble spots and beats in the story. Remember to talk out loud during your play with the ideas.

Word dancing journal
- What did you discover about changing the story from talking out loud?
- How do you examine and engage with the beats in this episode?
- In what way was this play different than simply talking out loud about what comes next in the story?

Note that additional exercises included here invite you to play with trouble spots in your story. Please adapt them to work with your story. Play out loud and do not worry about the chronological order of the questions or the story. Rethink, use your imagination, and engage with how tension can move your story-crafting and development.

Questions to Address when Working with Trouble

This series of exercises addresses how to recognize, increase, and decrease tension, thereby extending a story-crafter's range. Practice out loud with or without a partner. As in the previous exercises, I encourage the use of a word dancing journal for reflection. Write down what you discover. Guiding questions are provided for reflection.

Exercise One: Threefold Extension of the Conflict:

Purpose of the exercise—Examine the tension in the story by strategically rearranging the tension instead of the plot. Select three trouble or possible trouble points and increase the tension in a threefold manner. Look at the tension as something that can escalate from strong, to stronger, to strongest. It does not need to occur sequentially but instead, strategically. In fact, the more strategically you use tension, the less you need to worry about what happens in the story. Instead, concentrate on why it happens.

> *An Example:*
> In the story of "Jack and the Beanstalk", there are three possible trouble point areas: when Jack sells the cow for beans, when the giant discovers Jack and when the giant climbs down the beanstalk. Any one of these trouble spots can be intensified. For example, the giant's discovery of Jack may be explored in three increasing ways: (1) he smells Jack, and in your play, you explore how the pungent human scent is a telltale sign, (2) the giant hears a sneeze from the cupboard where Jack has been hiding, (3) the giant puts his glasses on, and now that he can see two times better than he did before, he finally sees Jack. This threefold extension of the tension helps to elevate the story in a playful and meaningful way.

Discuss out loud—Select three tensions or possible tension times in a story. Try to choose less obvious points of tension. This is so you can play with and discover new trouble spots that might appear in a threefold fashion. Tell the story three times. Each time you tell, increase the trouble by one level. By the time you have told the tale three times, you will have a threefold approach to illustrating the same story with different levels of complexity.

Word dancing journal
- What new discoveries did you find?
- How did you elevate the trouble?
- How could you take this exercise even further?

Exercise Two: Decreasing Tension to Discover new Tension

Purpose of the Exercise—In the first exercise, increasing the tension was the objective. In this exercise, recognizing tension points and decreasing the tension is the new objective. Story-crafting can build up and tear down significant episodes by increasing and decreasing story intensity. As noted earlier in the chapter, trouble drives the story. First, we will select three trouble or possible trouble points to play with. Then we will decrease the tension at these points in a threefold manner, by enhancing the tension so it is weak, weaker, and weakest. The tension decrease does not have to occur in sequence. In fact, it should become a more strategic part of the story.

For example:
In the "Jack and the Beanstalk" example, one trouble spot is when the giant climbs down the beanstalk after Jack. To decrease the tension and to lessen the intensity, three story choices the story-crafter can play with are: (1) to give Jack a sizable head start down the beanstalk so he has plenty of time to cut down the vine, (2) to have the giant be a bumbling oaf—awkward walking, poor eyesight, dim vocal control—so that it becomes clear that Jack will be the victor, and (3) Jack is able to assemble the town and recruit a small army to help him before the giant steps off of the beanstalk.

Decreasing the intensity changes the story. By playing with these ideas, other parts of the story will rise in significance.

Word dancing journal
- What did you discover when you decreased the tension?
- Were there any new tensions that you noticed?

- Explain how you decided to change these times?

Exercise Three: Shifting Tensions:

Purpose of the exercise—This exercise combines the previous two exercises by shifting the tensions. Shifting tensions can change story direction. Investment in a story occurs when there are changing elevations of intensity. This exercise helps the story-crafter play with the results of a scene by increasing and decreasing the intensity of the scene.

> *For example:*
> The giant was an oaf, but we find that when he puts his glasses is on, he was only clumsy because he could not see where he was going. Now with his glasses, the tension increases because the Giant is more likely to catch Jack. Increasing and decreasing the tensions invites play.

> *Word dancing journal*

- When you change the story to increase tension, do you find new beats?
- In any given change, one element increases, the other decreases. When increasing tension, what do you decrease to strengthen your tension moment? Record your thoughts.
- When changing the story to decrease tension, do you find new beats to the story?
- Was there a noticeable change occurring from decreasing the tension? Record your thoughts.

Exercise Four: French Doors

Purpose of the exercise—In dramatic circles, entrances or exits create tension—trouble—or possible trouble spots. A French door scene is a "... unit of action that begins and ends with the entrance or exit of a character." (Dunne, 2009 175) Examine how a character enters and exits. Drama experts such as Viola Spolin and Uta Hagan emphasize that entrances and exits are pivotal times for drama. The same significance is true with story. Play with not only the entering and exiting of standard characters, but also explore the possible impact of other characters' entrances and exits. By thinking out loud, you can invite new characters to enter and exit.

Discuss out loud—Tell the story and enhance each exit and entrance.

Pay particular attention to the dialogue created. Have a character exit from an episode unexpectedly. Pay close attention to what becomes heightened when you decrease the impact of the exit. Tell the story but make your character enter at three different nonscheduled times. How does the story change? Tell the story but make the character have different reasons for exiting. Tell the story but have an unknown person enter the story.

Word dancing journal
- What did you discover about how the characters interact with others?
- What was the scene with the most intensity?
- What happened when an unknown person exited?

Exercise Five: Unresolved action

Purpose of the Exercise—Stories are based on give and take situations. If a character is given a test, he or she chooses whether to take it. If a character is provided a parachute for jumping off of a mountain, again, he or she chooses to take it or not. The episode depends on actions and reactions. One event gives way so another builds. Story-crafting increases and releases these tensions. The story-crafter examines the unresolved parts of the story. Even the smallest unresolved item can carry weight. Consider a response to the following questions:

1. What is unresolved in the story? Why did I leave it unresolved?
2. Would it help the story to make it more significant and attempt to resolve it?
3. Who should resolve it?
4. How should I resolve it?
5. What is resolved that should remain unresolved?

Discuss out loud—Tell the story out loud, but only after addressing the above questions. Play with what might seem obvious to resolve and leave it—and vice versa. Test your new awareness and see what you can use in the story.

Word dancing journal
- Did you find any new resolutions from this work?
- What did you keep unresolved? Why?

- What new places did you find? What was a time that made you stop and rethink the story? Why? Explain.

Exercise Six: The Ticking Clock

Purpose of the exercise—This exercise allows the story to be played out under time restraints.

With a clock, watch, or stopwatch, tell your story, but have the trouble in the story resolved in a series of time markers. Start with two minutes, then go to one minute, then thirty seconds. Write down what you discovered.

Word dancing journal
- What did you leave out and what did you keep?
- What did this sense of urgency do to your energy?
- If you had just 30 more seconds, what more could you do?

Here are some other ways to explore increasing and decreasing trouble in your story.

1. *Take away something essential.* What would happen if the wolf was toothless? How would he compensate for the loss? Would he compensate?
2. *Raise the bar by increasing the danger of the story.* If Robin Hood does not rescue Maid Marion, she is not only placed in jail but she is beheaded. He has one hour to save her. What does he do?
3. *Place a traitor within the story.* In story, we can play with many ideas to see how the story changes when a traitor is revealed.
4. *Take away the hero's ability to defend him or herself.* What would happen if the dragon could no longer breathe fire? What would occur if the character Drink Well, from the Jack tale, could no longer swallow the ocean in one gulp or Zorro lost his sword? Make your main character more vulnerable.
5. *Use the unknown to create tension or anxiety.* What if Jack's mother is sick and he can't find a way to cure her? What if Red hears the sounds of three approaching wolves and not just one? Create tension by having the character struggle. Increase the struggle will help to produce more investment in the story. Decide when the breaking point occurs with the character's anxiety.

These are a few oral exercises to word dance with your story. Play with them and adapt your own. As you dance with your words, realize that while each move can be subtle or fierce, every choice moves the story. You can play with misdirection and intensity. Remember to dance. Dance with your words out loud, let the trouble bubble, emerge, and sit idle. Playing with trouble creates meaning. Use trouble as a creative tool to help you play.

Next Steps

We have discussed how we can trouble our stories. Now we will examine how we can enlist someone else to listen to our stories. As mentioned, deep listening is a critical requirement for effective story-crafting. The next chapter will outline how to first recognize a deep listener and how this can add to your work as a story-crafter. What will be discussed are methods to improve listening practices beyond listening to my story. This will help to provide a better collaborative environment for writing and telling stories.

Where should the word be found,
where will the word resound?
Not here, there is not enough silence.
—T. S. ELIOT, BRITISH/AMERICAN POET

Chapter 5
Deep Listening—Working with a Partner

Story-crafters often work alone, composing and creating material ready for print and/or telling. They cement thoughts, wrestle with new ideas, engage in the private practice of writing, and at times, drift into worries about family, friends, work, or schedules. Outside noise distracts them from the focus needed to make story come alive. Story-crafters need to concentrate, but frankly, things often interrupt their work.

Imagine someone who helps you focus and concentrate as you create, listening fully to your work and offering suggestions when asked. He or she alerts you to possible new directions and misdirections; guiding and filtering the outside noise to refocus your story work. Find a storytelling partner to deeply listen to your story play who is skilled—or trained—to block out the extraneous physical or internal noise. With the right mindset and a partner aligned in your story-based play, noises decrease.

Some people are paying attention to their own coaching techniques or strategies, already knowing what they want to say, and thus, not concentrating on your work as best they could. They are focusing on correcting before they truly understand the storytellers' needs. They see themselves as directors but undervalue listening before offering suggestions. This is not necessarily a fault of the partner; it takes work to create a deep listening focus. Unless someone makes this their first skill to refine, they will have a harder time with listening deeply. Some may listen more to story development instead of story flow. Deep listening develops through repeated practice and reflection. A partner must agree to consciously improve his or her listening ability to be a deep listener. The same rings true for the partner. They are shared roles. A storyteller partner should be someone who shares stories as well as listens to them. If they are also a story-crafter, they will understand the process of both teller and listener. Choose carefully when selecting a listening partner.

Recognizing the Importance of Listening

There are times when a boss, teacher, friend, or even a family member "phones in" that they are listening to what you are saying. One can tell by the lack of focus, the shifting of the feet, or the wandering eyes. As a speech and storytelling teacher, I had to learn this. I could not always focus on my students. I listened to my students tell stories. It was not uncommon to hear twenty to forty stories a day. I found myself drifting during some of the stories. By the time I had heard my fortieth folktale, I began thinking of something else. It took me awhile to realize that it served no purpose to listen when my focus was just not there. I would stop and say to the student something similar to,

> Your story is too important not to hear. I want to really listen to your story. Do you mind if we take a break so I can do just that? I need a few minutes to train my mind to focus on your story. I am drifting and I really want to hear what you have developed.

My students appreciated this honesty then and now, and often asked if I needed a break to listen deeper. When focusing, I could respond to what they were sharing with me. Together we gradually understood and used this concept of deep listening.

The Value of Having a Listening Partner

Story-crafters can use their time when working alone to refine, practice, revisit, and most of all, play with story. However, a partner invites new awareness to this play. Having someone to really concentrate on the story allows the teller to concentrate on the tale. Their focus can be on the delivery and even how they are feeling while telling it. For example, when writing/telling a British folktale, the story-crafter can align their thinking with sharing the tale. He or she can explore with the story-crafter three new story endings to discover the best fit. Your partner listens, the crafter shares. The listener puts the story and telling in focus while the story-crafter continues orally working on the story. A partner can also record and reflect on the experience. The teller does not have to stop the story.

Story Silence

A deep listener pays attention to what is said and not said. Silence and stillness move story in ways sound cannot. An abrupt pause before someone says, "I made a mistake" or "He is not my son" speaks volumes. A partner focuses on story sound and silence as tools of the story-crafter, inviting decisions and creativity that might alter a story's direction.

What is Deep Listening?

Trust creates deep listening. Storyteller and coach Marni Gillard, author of *Storyteller, Storyteacher* (1996), shares her knowledge online at www.youthstorytelling.com:

> I find out how to help through deep listening. I listen wholeheartedly. I nod, laugh and grimace. I offer what Pam McGrath calls "a juicy face." I wait out a long pause with relaxed patience. I know even experienced tellers; working with a new tale, struggle to capture an image in words. I look and listen for the nuances of a teller's style. When anyone is listened too deeply, he is more likely to give that gift to others. … When I listen well, I hear many things. As a coach, I focus on the teller's hopes for the tale. Does this take time? Yes. But when I just give quick tips, I'm more copy editor than coach. (n.d.)

Deep listening invites trusting each other. A deep listener might hear something the story-crafter did not because he or she focuses more on sharing the story. The listener might find new places for pauses, suggest a new character direction, or even comment on possible alternative endings. Listeners might offer choices the story-crafter should have made, instead of the ones that happened.

The story experience is both contextual and personal; no one formula will serve all. Sometimes the reason someone shares a story is revealed from deep listening. A story-crafter might be sharing a tale about your sister because she misses her and one way that she deals with this is to create a story about her. The reason for telling is that she is engaged in a personal search to become closer to a sister. A deep listening experience will reveal this. One of my students once said to me, "every story you tell has a little bit of you in it." This is important for listeners to keep in mind. Sometimes the teller does not want to share the rationale for the story or why he or she is crafting it. They may not know it themselves, but if the teller seeks out a listening partner who works hard to personally know the story-crafter and his or her work, there will be more trust and more in-depth opportunities to share in the story's development.

Deep listening drives play. Thoreau shares, "It takes two to speak the truth—one to speak and another to hear." Story success develops from the rich conversation before, during, and after the story is told. The talk of the teller steers the truth for the listening, requiring a partnership between teller and partner to develop negotiated direction for story ideas.

In order to develop effective deep listening, I have written down parameters of listening that will enable the best experience. Following these and developing them over time will ensure success and concentration as a deep listener.

Parameters of Listening

Active concentration on more than words and also examining how the words work in connection with the teller. A listening partner doesn't simply listen for word choice, instead they experience the journey created from the chosen words. The volume of the words, the placement of the teller, and the hand motions, all reveal the storyteller's journey. The listening partner pays careful attention sharing concrete and specific feedback, alerting the story-crafter to heighten or decrease significant sections of the story or trouble spots based on his or her perspective. Quality feedback for the story-crafter can be powerful. For example:

> What made the creature seem eerie was the strength in your
> voice, especially when it was growling at the fox. I could hear
> how mad he was by the pitch in your voice. It sounded like

pebbles in a jar. Plus, I don't know if you realized it, but your fingers formed claws, which only made it more believable. This also answers why I was even more scared. It was because of the way your hands reached out when you said, "You never know what to expect."

The listener responds with detail. Instead of, "I could see the dress", they could share, "I could see the rich, velvet red dress. For me it was not ironed. It looked a little shaggy and it made me wonder who made it?" The listener responds not in general word statements, but instead shares the pictures that were unfolding as he or she heard the story. These images offer pictorial feedback and often include guiding questions, demonstrating rich listening. Listening is an active process. These exchanges and conversations direct the story, inviting the listener to rethink his or her decisions. Storytelling is vastly different from simple observation. A story listener shares what he or she sees with the purpose of inviting further conversation. It is not simply to appreciate what he or she sees, but instead to focus on what they can see and witness in their own mind from the experience.

The teller focuses on sharing the story. The teller lives in the moment, not focusing on the story's polish but simply telling the tale. The teller shares the story, not concerned with how to lean in to accentuate closeness to the audience or how to turn their body to show fear; they simply do it. A deep listener takes notes and uses this to begin the reflective discussion afterwards. To reconsider a story, the listener asks questions like, "Did you realize your whole body shifted closer to me when the wolf was approaching?"

Listeners can also respond to how something sounded as the teller told it:

Did you know that your voice sounded as small as a mouse when Hilda was trapped under the floorboard? This is something you might remember when she is trapped later in the other house under the stairs.

A deep listener can also respond by asking to hear something again, suggesting changes during the retelling. "When the girl is trapped under the floorboard, you might consider starting with a smaller sound and then raising your voice as she gets closer to you?" The language is suggested for improvement but shared with sensitivity.

A deep listener serves as a second eye and/or ear. They share what they hear, how it might be improved. Most of all, they listen to what the teller needs and work from there. They do not discount the teller's needs or suggestions.

The Power of Questions:

The British writer and educator Aidan Chambers advises that when asking children to clarify points on their story, avoid asking "why." Instead, simply say "tell me." He reasons that by asking why, we limit the child to respond only to the question, where as, "tell me" invites the child to share more of the story he or she is composing. The same applies to the work of the story-crafter. Chambers states, "Most of us do not know what we think until we hear what we said" (1996 97). Instead of explaining, both listener and teller retell the story. In telling the story or parts of the story again, they can add to the teller and experience it again. Unless a story is memorized, we choose different words when we retell. This also creates a new emotional experience. "Tell me more about the bear hiding in the forest." "Tell me about Daisy not liking her mother." "Tell me about the choices Arthur could take as a king." These simple words invite the teller to paint the story with emotional words and experience the story again in a new way. We could ask "why is this person doing this?" But then the response is confined to address questions, rather, "tell me" invites a narrative. For story-crafting, this is an effective request when working with narrative development.

Work to Stay Focused when Listening

Initially, focus can be difficult, but rewarding over time. It takes practice. Spend the first five, but no more than ten minutes, talking without judgment and listening without editorializing. The teller and the listener can discuss what is bothering them so that it does not affect the story-crafting work ahead.

> "But what I like doing best is Nothing." "How do you do nothing?" asked Pooh, after he had wondered for a long time. "Well, it's when people call out at you just as you're going off to do it, What are you going to do Christopher Robin, and you say, Oh, nothing, and you go and do it." "Oh, I see," said Pooh. "This is a Nothing sort of thing that we're doing right now." "Oh, I see," said Pooh again. "It means just going along,

listening to all the things you can't hear and not bothering."
"Oh!" said Pooh." (Milne & Shepard 1961)

Too often tellers simply rush to the story without realizing the value of clearing their minds before beginning. A story-crafter's mind needs to be clear to engage in play. As the creator of the popular *Calvin and Hobbes*, cartoonist Bill Watterson said, "Letting your mind play is the best way to solve problems." (1990). Storycrafters should be prepared to play, but they need to voice their tension to someone before they can play. As Natalie Goldberg, author of *Writing down the Bones* reminds, "stress is an ignorant state. It believes everything is an emergency" (1986). A story-crafter needs to work to lessen this emergency by talking it out. Stress remains even after your story-crafting experience—hopefully it may be reduced. Create a practice of release.

When listening strength is low, create time for breaks to build listening skills. Both partners must feel comfortable enough to initiate break time. It is okay to pause, and return with greater strength. Informal conversations can further the direction of your story work or simply provide the rest needed to begin again with fresh eyes.

Refrain from comment until asked. This may be difficult because story-crafters like to talk, but authors need to make mistakes and be free to share them while telling. They also need to feel free to stop and write down ideas. If they know you are only deeply listening, they feel more relaxed about sharing. Deep listening develops from commitment and practice. As a warm up, ask your listening partner to pay attention to what you had for breakfast as you recall the experience without interrupting. Try listening to a mundane topic such as, what the teller had for breakfast. Practice until both partners are comfortable with the process. Too often, a coach or listener listens with the intent of "fixing," offering comments and breaking the story's rhythm and flow. This approach shifts the focus to listener and not the teller. Listening free of comments keeps the teller in charge. This is precious time. Let it unfold.

Do not rush. Story-crafting with a partner is an investment not fully realized in a matter of minutes. Reserve quality time to share, revisit, and re-experience the story. It is worth the time. It is sometimes after a period of practice that discoveries are often made and sometimes these discoveries occur by accident. A story-crafter needs to let the process develop and this can only happen after a consistent amount of time. Rushing the process produces rushed results.

Believe in the value and power of deep listening. Commit to this work. A story-crafter releases inhibitions about the practice. It is important to note that this process has worked for countless people for thousands of years. The principles of Zen are based on deep listening practices. The practice builds better stories both for publication and for telling. Trust in the work and your partner, letting the experience grow each time, through inviting change and improvement.

As Eudora Welty reveals in *One Writer's Beginnings* (1984):

> Long before I wrote stories, I listened for stories. Listening for them is something more acute than listening to them. I suppose it's an early form of participation in what goes on. Listening children know stories are there. When their elders sit and begin, children are just waiting and hoping for one to come out, like a mouse from its hole. (14)

Like the curious mouse, sniff out the stories your partner reveals through his or her verbal and nonverbal words and actions. Stories are hidden in the corner, behind doors, tucked away in blankets, and even in the mouths of dragons. Deep listeners help story-crafters reveal these treasures.

Commit to Continual Listening Practice.

Both the teller and listener will experience dramatic growth from continual practice and reflection. It is recommended, to practice weekly or at the least, biweekly. Remember, story-crafters are developing a partner to whom to tell and listen to their craft, and not a simply to tell a story to. Instead, seek out a partner or partners who can work to develop who you are as a narrative developer.

Within the parameters of deep listening, there are specific ways to listen. More than simple feedback, these methods focus listening to attend to specific needs and directions. Outlined below are specific ways to listen to a story and directions for responding to a story-crafter's narrative.

1. *Listen to the whole story.* The listener deeply listens to the entire story—or as much as the teller wants to share—only

then offering comments. This is the traditional method of listening. This is the style most often found in storytelling circles. However, in this work, the listener also suggests possible directions the teller might use with play. For example, the listener might say, "I heard the story as you told it and I like the part when the wolf starts out cruel but changes. However, you might consider playing with how the wolf changes to be less cruel. Why not play this out and record the ideas from the play?" Instead of simply making suggestions about the story, the deep listener suggests other ways the story can be shaped by using playful exercises.

2. *Listen to the significant moment of the story.* Ask the teller, "What is the significant moment in the story?" Noted story coach Doug Lipman calls this the "MIT" or most important thing (1999). The most important thing drives the story and has to be included. Determine why the significant moment is critical. Ask the teller what he or she believes precedes or follows this moment. Then ask the story-crafter to share at least three retellings that highlight the significance of the story. The listener then writes down responses to the stories. The comments can be used to further conversation about deepening the story significance.

3. *Listen to the introduction and conclusion.* Ask the teller to share the beginning and the end of the story. Make sure each part lasts about two to four minutes. Discuss the strength of word choice. Talk about the importance of this significance. When the listener only hears the beginning and end, he or she can imagine how the middle part does or does not fit. They might talk out the main points of the middle of the tale working with the introduction and conclusion. The teller records what is said and decides whether or not to use it.

4. *Listen for the actions of one character.* In this exercise, the listening partner focuses on the actions, dialogue, and nonactions of a chosen character. The partners provide feedback notes for the teller. Basically the teller shares his or her story, but the listener focuses on one character and how he or she serves the story. They can examine what the character does or does not do—non-action—of the character. For example, the listener can say he or she noticed people in the story who are worried that they will go to jail and not be

provided proper representation. Did we forget that Andrew is a part-time lawyer? Might he offer up his services? Could we play with this idea? Together the teller and listener reflect on how and why one character reacts and moves in the story. The teller cannot do this kind of work alone. Adding a listener can help the teller revisit a certain character. A possible conversation might begin, "The ogre was angry when he met the archer, but he ran away when first meeting him. Do you think this is a logical reaction for an ogre who is meant to scare others?" These types of conversations can help the story-crafter revisit the character. This same type of discovery can be repeated for the environment, a secondary character, a certain plot point or any other significant elements.

5. *Listen for the senses.* How the senses—hearing, sight, smell, touch, taste—work in the story can help accentuate a story. The teller retells the story concentrating on only one sense; highlighting this sense in the story. The teller works to make one sense more dominant. For example, in retelling the story of *Little Red Riding Hood,* the story-crafter concentrates on how smell acts in the story. In recalling the grandmother, talk about how Red knew her because she wore her favorite fragrance, lilac and her cotton dress smelled old. Then, share how the wolf was pungent and when he showed Red his teeth, it smelled like he had not brushed them in months. Then switch to a new sense. Touch the grandmother's hands that felt like old railroad spikes. They were always cold and well-worn. The wolf's fur felt like an old coat that her mother threw on the floor like a rug in the back room. All this sensory-concentrated work can take the story in new directions.

6. *Listen for what is said and not said.* Invite the listener to create two columns on a piece of paper—one for what is said, the other for what is not said. For example, your character said, "I want to gobble you up!" But what the character did not say is "Why?" You said, "We are lost," but you did not say why the characters were lost. Add a third column to suggest what else might help the story based upon what was said or not said. You said, "We are lost," but perhaps instead of directly saying we are lost, can you show it by letting the listener see it. "Every step he took he traveled farther away from what he knew." You could say, "I want to gobble you up!" But rather, show this by the character licking his lips and remarking how hungry he is.

So much can be developed from the unspoken. The unspoken can rise to the surface when a deep listener creates focus.

7. *Listen for the silences.* The teller finds three to five places to introduce a dramatic pause into the story reflecting on why these choices were made. Silence creates power in story, but is often overlooked. Play with silence to create meaningful pauses, but also stress how sounds are used. Playing with dramatic pauses can help highlight significance to the tale.

8. *Listen for color.* Ask the teller to share the story, but highlight one specific color in the story. However, remember that attached to color is mood and writers often use color as metaphor. The dark sky made me feel terrible. The bright yellow rays of the sun informed me that the morning has started. Color can help create a desired effect. In the first telling, ask the teller to share as many colors as they can when telling the story. The listener writes down what colors are used and how they are used. They have a discussion about the use. Now tell the story again, but only highlight one color when telling the story. Does the story change when this happens? What is the emotional impact from the story using one color? Play with the range of colors.

9. *Listen for the possible and impossible.* The teller listens for those moments that are not possible or unresolved. The great thing about playing with story-crafting is that one can play with the nontraditional or impossible. For example, in the story of "Jack and the Beanstalk", it is not said or expected that Jack finds a new set of beans and is able to grow them as tall as the giant. This changes the story. Sometimes working with these ideas can help the story-crafter to find new directions for his or her story development. The teller can break the rules of the fiction. For example, Rapunzel cannot leave the castle until her prince rescues her. However, what if she finds a secret door to the second level of the castle? She has a chance to escape without the prince. Would her exit strategy change? What does this say for the prince's role? Play with your deep listening partner to determine how the impossible can be possible. Sometimes it is inviting to step out of traditional choices.

10. *Listen and react, listen and react.* The teller shares a portion of the story. When the listener responds, "react," the teller stops to share his or her reaction to what is happening. These

discoveries might find their way into the story. This continues to help break the formulaic rhythm of the story so that more playful and creative ways to study the story's development can be examined. As ancient Greek rhetorician Isocrates states, "Spend your leisure time in cultivating an ear attentive to discourse, for in this way you will find that you learn with ease what others have found out with difficulty." Play advances story-crafting.

All of these methods employ playful new ways and roles for the listener to heighten the teller's understanding of his or her craft. Let the art speak so others can listen. As writer Madeline L'Engle shares, "When the work takes over, then the artist is enabled to get out of the way, not to interfere. When the work takes over, then the artist listens." (1980) Listening helps us understand the process of story-crafting. When we share this process with someone else, the possibilities are endless and the experience is richly improved.

In the next chapter, I introduce a special type of coaching that I call story mediation. This is a unique practice that helps the teller or tellers by stepping inside the world of the story with the tellers. It is a dynamic method to improve our practice as story-crafters.

Chapter 6
Mediation and Co-Creating Stories

Authors, storytellers, writers, and other imaginative thinkers usually share their narratives only once, when complete—although they often wrestle with many attempts to produce a finished product. It is misleading to believe work must be "ready" before it is shared. Work in progress can be revisited, adapted, or changed, and in a greater sense, become a tool for play. Exploration creates a safe space and invites others' perspectives and insights without threat, to forge new directions. Writers and tellers can wrestle with each other's ideas, suggestions, and concerns, collaborating, rewriting, retelling, and rethinking the story's possibilities.

Traditionally, when working with a partner on a narrative, the teller or writer shares the story, while the listener takes notes providing feedback. However, it is not enough to tell a story to a partner and then wait for suggestions. The most effective story coaches place the needs of the teller/writer first creating a deep listening relationship. The listener searches for verbal and nonverbal story delivery.

Throughout my career, I have been coached by a variety of storytellers including Doug Lipman, Marni Gillard, the late Chuck Larkin, and a host of many other known and not-so-known tellers. Each experience helped build my personal coaching style as I stood on the shoulders of these talented and caring coaches. Lipman and Gillard emphasized reflection. At times, Larkin could be abrupt but was always honest in his comments. Each coach cared in different ways. Larkin provided uncensored, yet caring remarks while at other times he would be a warm listener as my ideas took shape. This circle of care created a trusting relationship and allowed me to proceed in new directions in my story work.

In working with Lipman and Gillard, I wrote a kid's story about missing my father who worked at Goodyear Tire and Rubber Company for over twenty-five years. However, in the personal coaching work, I discovered my story was also about how I was torn between serving more adult roles in my father's absence at a young age.

Their gentle, guiding questions helped me discover the inherent whys. They helped me to focus on why I felt the way I did when my dad was away and how I took on adult roles when he was not there. They created a safe place for me to comfortably share within a group why I had written the tale and what I was hoping to tell in this story. They did not judge me. Instead, their reflective questions and comments invited me to see inside the story. Together we discovered what I needed for the story to work.

Discovery is valuable and worthwhile and this can occur when trained listeners become coaches or as I call them, story mediators. This chapter addresses a different form of coaching that I call story mediation. Working with a partner, or later in a group, the listener does more than deep listening; they find a place to enter the story as it is being told. The story mediator works with the teller to explore the story as though it was happening as they tell it. It requires imaginative thinking and safe risk taking on the part of the teller.

Tellers Partner on a Story not Finished—A Work in Progress—Explore the Rich Depth both Inside and Outside the Story

Together story partners dig deeper into the story-crafting process drawing from what Lipman called "thinking in the present" defined, "to include not just conscious, analytical thought, but also unconscious, intuitive, nonlinear forms of thinking" (1999 12). Mediation is more than thinking in the present. Tellers step inside the present world of the story playing in real time. "Storytelling requires you to imagine the stories you tell" (47). More than imagining, mediators act on their imaginations, and in a real sense, allow the story to unfold as though they were in it.

Although new to storytellers and writers, imaginative enactment has prevailed in drama, namely process or educational drama, for many years. Drama practitioners such as Dorothy Heathcote, Cecily O'Neil, Brian Edmiston, Rives Collins, and David Booth have extended this pedagogy of practice rooted in story and drama.

Heathcote is considered the pioneer of process drama; this is a method, according to Schneider & Jackson (2000) that is

> … a method of teaching and learning that involves students in imaginary, unscripted, and spontaneous scenes. Process drama exists through the interactions of students and teachers, and is framed by curriculum topics, teacher objectives, and student's personal experiences. (quoted in O'Neill, 1995; Rogers & O'Neill, 1993)

This work involves students and the teacher working together in the creation of a fictional world. In this world, they enact and engage in order to learn something that exists in this world. However, they do not enter the world as students and teachers. Instead, they enter the fiction by taking on roles of people they are invested in. In this world of the fiction, they use roles to negotiate the world. They take on roles as Heathcote states as though they were experts. Imagination is the key. In process drama, students and teachers work within the same fictional world. The teacher is the only one required to be in the fictional world and the classroom. This is so he or she can mediate and use drama to help reflect both inside and outside of the fictional world with the students. Roles are not determined, but emerge based from the drama created or from the inquiry based on the teacher's mediation. As Edmiston states,

> In process drama, participants use their social and cultural imagination to create a shared imagined world. The imagined world does not replace the everyday classroom world, but rather begins to be created alongside the everyday world. Teacher and students interact in both worlds simultaneously and as necessary they move back and forth between them at will. (2012)

Let me illustrate with an example.

> When I entered the class at Northwestern University, I did not know I would be actively engaged in history. The chairs

and tables were scattered in small, what was revealed to be stations, around the room. There were pictures about the Wild West covering the desks and chairs. Rives Collins, the professor, read an advertisement to us, not as the professor, but as someone recruiting people to walk on The Oregon Trail. In role, he shared that he was looking for new travelers to go with him. As a group, also in role, we chose to travel with him. We debated what to leave and what to keep for the journey. At each station, we found out something new about our journey. Along the journey, we created our narratives. Some people shared that they ate spoiled food and needed to do something. Others shared their expertise, fixing wagon wheels, cooking food, and watching for Indians. We faced real world decisions of the time and when some of us became sick we had to decide whether to leave them.

We did not tell a story; we lived it. The story was built from our ability to improvise and this story unfolded as we made decisions together. As Heathcote states,

> Improvisation … means "discovering by trial, error, and testing; using available materials with respect for their nature, and being guided by the appreciation of their potential." The "end product" of improvisation is the experience of it. (1984 45)

It is the experience that builds the students' learning. They are not passively watching the story. They are actively engaged in making it happen.

The Experience of Storytelling

Could story-crafters use this method or a variation to assist storytellers, writers, and other imaginative thinkers to dig more deeply into their narratives? By applying dramatic and playful improvisation, story-crafters can take their stories to the next level. Using improvisation helps story-crafters experience and explore their work within a deeper context.

Deep listening helps us think about the experience of the story. Trouble elevates the story.

> Trouble is the engine of narrative and the justification for going public with a story. It is the whiff that leads us to search

out the relevant or responsible constituents in the narrative, in order to convert the raw Trouble into a manageable problem that can be handled with procedural muscle. (Bruner. 1991 12)

Using drama to explore story-based trouble will assist the teller to play with the stories. Before explaining and demonstrating how this works, it becomes necessary to become familiar with some terms used in story mediation.

Terms

Story mediation—The partner actively works to connect ideas and explore the teller's interest in playful, dramatic story-based practices. This can include stepping inside the world of the storyteller or even imagining and entertaining possible routes for the story in partnership with the teller. The teller paints the story creating a playground for meditation, imagination, and enactment (Cordi 2011).

Side coaching—Drama specialist Viola Spolin first introduced this coaching technique, inviting the actor, or this is case, the story-crafter, to improvise the moment of the story. It is a method, "in holding the student-actor to the point of concentration when he may have wandered away … and keeps him functioning at a fresh moment of experience." (1963 3-4). It is this freshness of experience that is most important. Side coaching allows the actor—or teller—to stay in the moment of their work, while the coach—or mediator—suggests new story choices.

How does this side coaching work with story-crafting? Initially created for actors, side coaching applies to the work of the story-crafter as well. In story-crafting, the story mediator is the person who side coaches the teller. Spolin warns, "… Great care must be taken to see that it does not disintegrate into an approval/disapproval involvement instead a command to be obeyed!" (1963 4-6) The coaching purpose is to use play to help the teller to engage in the storytelling world he or she is creating.

Improvisation

This is more than a tool: it is a disciplined practice used to act and react to the fictional now. The actor—or teller—reacts to the event as though it was occurring at the present time. "The intuitive can only respond in immediacy of right now. It comes bearing its gifts in the moment of spontaneity, the moment when we are freed to relate and act, involving ourselves in the moving, changing world around us." (Spolin, 1963 6-7). It occurs in spontaneous times. As Spolin states,

> Spontaneity is the moment of personal freedom when we are faced with a reality and see it, explore it and act accordingly. In this reality the bits and pieces of ourselves function as an organic whole. It is the time of discovery, of experiencing, of creative expression. (6)

How does improvisation work with story-crafting? The emphasis for the story mediator is that the teller experiences the story. A mediator draws from the planned and unplanned ideas that arise from the experience. In order to create the experience, the story mediator employs playful exercises, side coaching, and reflective questioning with the teller. The teller should feel the personal freedom to fail with the story, but at the same time, take risks that bring newness to the story.

Role—Role in story mediation, as well as in process drama, differs from performed theatre. It is used to invest in the story. A story-crafter can take on many roles to see and experience the story from multiple perspectives. This is a new lens with which to experience the work. Dorothy Heathcote said that if students want to study a subject, we should place them in role. They should take on a "Mantle of the Expert" (1994 5). The same applies to the teacher. When a person assumes an expert position, they see and experience the world as that expert. This can be achieved by using role.

How does role work with story-crafting? A *teacher-in-role* challenges classroom students to form new perspectives and inquire about the subjects they are exploring. Heathcote introduced teacher-in-role where the teacher mediates or directs the fictional world based on inquiry. With attribution to Heathcote, I share what I call *storyteller-in-role* (Cordi 2012). Like teacher-in-role, this is the process where the storyteller or the mediator working within the story uses role to examine a deeper idea about the story. This is different from assigning a role; this is a pedagogical process to use role to examine issues or ideas within the story. A mediator might ask the storyteller to be the wolf although they have only considered Little Red's perspective. However, the roles could quickly shift and the mediator may take on the role within the story as the huntsman or have the teller voice what the huntsman might be thinking. These playful practices using role help the teller invest and enter the fictional world. The story mediator also can use role to help the teller invest in the narrative. The mediator can heighten story tension. As Red's mother, the mediator might use role to change time in the story. The mediator might enact a time when Red might be entering school for the first time where she learns to not talk to strangers. This work with role might help the story-crafter see the story differently than simply telling the story. Heathcote (1984) said of role, "… that it is unpremeditated, unplanned, and therefore constantly can surprise the individual into new awareness" (51). A story mediator skillfully uses role to engage with the fictional world with the teller.

Jumping in and Out of the Story

As the story mediator listens and responds to the teller, he or she searches for entry places to jump in to help illuminate or clarify the story. At the same time, the mediator must carefully choose to jump out of the story to illustrate an idea or take the story in new directions.

Receiving feedback without breaking the flow of the story is rewarding, but with mediation, the teller can see, envision, talk out loud, and even use drama to engage in the ever-changing created world. Each time, the feedback can help mediate the process, often seeing and exploring the story in a new way.

Steps to Story Mediation

In order to understand the most effective ways to use this pedagogical process, I have outlined a series of steps to follow to ensure that story mediation works.

Start with an invitation. Because story mediation differs from story coaching, ask the teller if he or she is willing to engage in playful exercises with story in a way to which they are not accustomed. Share with them that although this is new, it is safe. Explain that in this work you are willing to explore different story directions not yet planned. Much of the original story line can be suspended to discover different possibilities. It is not essential to tell the whole story. Instead, concentrate on story segments or even exercises to continue understanding the environment.

> Working with fifth graders on the story of "Jack and the Beanstalk," I asked "what if the giant had a brother? How would he feel about Jack?" I then invited them to explore what would happen if we talked with Jim, the giant's brother. Another time I was working with teens and adults. We were studying the small village of Eyam in England that sacrificed the whole town so that the Black Plague would not spread throughout Europe. I then invited them to travel with me to the time when they discussed this plan with the mayor.

Explain and model side coaching. Side coaching is a powerful tool for story mediation. When Viola Spolin employed side coaching for actors, she used this method, but she only provided short sentences such as "Stay in the moment" or "Make it bigger". When the teller employs side coaching in story mediation more than a few sentences are used to keep the focus. The story mediator can side coach the teller to change the scene or even introduce a new character.

> When working with the kids as they were in the world of "Jim and the Beanstalk," along with the adults, we informed them that Jack's mother was sick and that they needed money to cure her. Jack was torn between stealing from Jim's gold coin collection or following his mother's rules not to steal. I then side coached a young boy who, with the class, had taken the coin and was not considering returning it. Using flashback and side coaching, I said on three we will return to the scene of Jack's mother telling him not to steal. Using side coaching, we did not stray from the fictional world, I simply changed it by introducing another perspective in the fiction.

> In working with the adults and teens, I will never forget that at the mayor's meeting we decided, in role, who must be saved for the sake of the community and who must not. One quiet teen, in role, began speaking about how crazy it was to decide one life over another. They said the blacksmith was old and, in order to preserve others, he must be sacrificed.

> Again using side coaching, I began to have the adults and teens

share, in role, the life of the blacksmith. From this fictional mediation, each person showed the compassionate, gentle nature of the blacksmith. Others told of his charity and how he took care of his mother when she was dying. After this, it was harder to carelessly say his life should end. We used side coaching to move the adults and teens to feel empathy for human life.

In side coaching, it is most important to stay in the moment, as Heathcote notes, the immediacy of right now. Staying in story, the changes that are made occur inside the narrative and move the story mediation into the fictional world.

However, people are not familiar with this process. I ask them to warm up to this method by telling me their morning routine and to not stop sharing unless I say the words "stop and look at me." These are the only times the person steps out of the narrative they are sharing. Initially we do fun activities like "Tell it faster," "Change the response as if you had an endless supply of biscuits and gravy" or "Share it like you would to a three-year-old." These exercises seem trivial, but in addition to helping the teller become comfortable with side coaching, the first saying of "tell it faster," frees the teller from a regular speaking rate and helps him or her experiment with a different tone.

These requests require the teller to trust the mediator. Since he or she is eating an endless supply of biscuits and gravy, they cannot quit the narrative; they need to stay in the moment. They are not following a script, but instead letting new narratives emerge from the side coaching. When I ask the story-crafter to "Share it like you would to a three-year-old," he or she needs to take this suggestion and change it to meet the new audience of young children. This changes their language structure as they are sharing new words and rhythms of language set for smaller audiences. All of these exercises can be fruitful when working the story.

Ask questions that frame the story. A story mediator does not want to immediately jump into a story. They first listen to find an entry point. Jumping in means finding a place where the mediator and the story-crafter can enter the fictional world together. The mediator will ask questions, and based on the responses, develop a better understanding of the narrative. Deeply listening, the mediator asks reflective questions to help both the teller and mediator see and clarify the story. However, the mediator also searches for backstories, and/or possible characters to explore, hidden or possible trouble, and even attitudes within the story. The teller's responses determine how to invest in the story.

Possible Questions to Promote Inquiry

At this point it is important to:

1. *Ask open-ended questions* to encourage narrative responses. Instead of asking "why," borrow a strategy from Aidan Chambers (1996) and ask for a story in response. The words "tell me" invite the teller to revisit and retell.

2. *Avoid asking for a plot summary.* Instead, ask the teller questions. Side coach to take the story in new directions. With the "Jim and the Beanstalk" experience, I asked about what would be the daily routine of a giant? From these questions, we explored the daily tasks of the giant, which helped the teller to connect more. A soundscape is where the teller makes the sounds they would hear in the fictional environment. The story mediation did not ask for what happened in the story—plot—but instead made attempts to better connect with the environment of the fiction.

3. *Avoid being predictable* Although tellers know their stories and are prepared to tell them, this is not always beneficial in story mediation. The mediator wants to help the teller explore new direction and ideas. Invite unpredictability as you mediate. Look for backstories. As mentioned, when working with the village of Eyam, we fleshed out the life of the blacksmith in order to understand that a person's position does not merit whether he or she should be sacrificed or not. Each person in stories has more to tell. Sometimes traveling using story mediation to the past or future times of the character can be unpredictable yet valuable, when explored. Don't underestimate how fleshing out the unknown in a story can help build the narratives.

4. *Look for pivotal times* in the story that need more investment. As the teller discusses the story, the mediator can search for parts of the story to explore. In the tale of Jim, Jack's brother, and the beanstalk, I could tell the students with whom I was working did not personally relate to the mother. In order to improve the connection, I created a letter that she wrote to

him when he was sick. This helped the students to become empathic toward the mother. In any given narrative, the story-crafter can dig deeper into an action or idea. The story mediator helps negotiate the significant times to explore.

5. *Search for how and why situations.* Story-crafters can invest more when we ask how and why. Asking how and why type questions invite story-crafters to reflect on the actions or character moves in the story. In the Eyam drama, a student spoke up in role dramatically questioning why one life is better than another. He began to ask what right they had to decide life and death. From this inquiry and reflective question, our narratives were stronger. How and why are door hinges upon which a story swings. Sometimes it is important to see how these doors hold up by questioning how strong the hinges are.

Jumping into the Story

While critical questions can help the teller inquire further into their stories, the heart of the work comes when the story mediator and teller engage in the fictional world. During the time the teller is asking questions, he or she is actively seeking out a place to move the questions from occurring outside the fictional world to inside the fictional world. This is a place where the story mediator asks,

- If we enter this time right now, would we learn something new?
- Is this a part that needs clarification; is there a way we could enact the story to make it clearer?
- In what way could studying behind the scenes help the narrative?
- Is this a complicated time with enough tension to move inside the story?

Initially, in the "Jim and the Beanstalk" story drama, I asked students what we knew about Jack from the beanstalk tale. Then, I asked the students what remains a mystery in the story? What do we still wonder about that was not resolved? Students began talking about working on a farm. When I asked more about what it meant to work on the farm, many of the city students did not have much recollection. As the story mediator, this was a telltale sign that

I either needed to move the story into the city or jump in to help them explore farming. After inviting them to be on the farm, I built the tension of the cow not providing milk. We used this event to jump into the fiction. Students, in role as farmers, asked inside the fiction, what is the best way to produce milk? How do you handle a cow? We also began moving inside this world. The students dramatically demonstrated trying to produce milk from the cow. They took on role of master farmer who knew more about duties on the farm. Some students became hungry chickens, which was a new tension we needed to resolve. After they worked in this fictional world for a while, I was able to jump in another world with them that included Jack and Jim, the giant on a farm.

When the story mediator jumps into the story during the crafting process, look for the following:

Unresolved issues: During reflection, explore a topic that needs to be resolved. Is there a character's interaction that needs to be explored more? In the Eyam drama, using story mediation each character provided his or her backstory. A young woman who worked as a merchant was viewed as more than a merchant. She was also a caretaker for three children. One character saw the mayor's inner thoughts when we voiced them to hear how worried he was about helping the town he was serving. These meaningful playful experiences helped see the community not as occupations but as people who serve many roles.

Minor characters might serve a bigger role. Many witness the story. Working with a teller on a story set in Las Alamos, New Mexico, the teller revealed several guards questioning why she and her friend were trying to crawl under the fence. I increased the trouble as a guard pointing out the clearly marked sign and penalty for crawling under the fence. This freed the teller to talk to the guard and not worry about the story. She began to understand how her character acted when she was defensive and even protective of her friend.

Disposition of the teller: When sharing, the teller's manner and behavior can help to read the needs of the story and the teller. Remember, one needs to make sure the story-crafter is comfortable with the work. Sometimes the nonverbal speaks louder than the verbal.

Ways to engage the teller

Restatement—Simply repeating what the teller has said, both in and out of role, helps the teller envision and engage with the story.

Repetition—Sometimes the story-crafter needs to hear what they have said. It helps them remember poignant points in the story and identify areas that might need more focus. However, skillful repeating can help direct new awareness.

Enactment of the voice—Skillfully use a voice of the character to help move the fiction. Say words in role to help focus the story on that character. This might be something said in the fiction or something that could have been said in the fiction.

Delivery—The way you decide to work in role can help the teller know more about the story.

Jumping Out Places for Clarity or Question

A story mediator may need to leave the story. The deeper we listen to a story, the more sensitive we become to the teller's needs. Sometimes stories take us too close to our experience, and we realize that we are in the world of the story when we are not ready to be there at this time. The story mediator needs to be a caretaker. Another time to jump out might simply be to transition from one story moment to another or even take a break. This type of mediation can be exhausting or cathartic. Sometimes taking a break will help the teller take it in. When mediating, these are the steps to follow. They can change based on the experience.

Spotlight on Story Mediation from *Hear Women Tell* Podcast

I asked Kris Hillenburg, the other half of *Hear Women Tell* podcasts on storytelling, to partake in story mediation with me. She hosts a monthly podcast that illuminates the value of storytelling. You can hear this process at www.herewomentell.com. Although she was apprehensive about this process, she engaged in it. I asked her to comment on this experience so you can experience it as she did—this type of story mediation can occur over the phone and in person—there is strength in each experience. You can hear my story mediation with Kris at http://www.herewomentell.com/archives/archives .html. Please look for my name.

Kris shares her experience.
When Kevin mentioned doing story mediation with me

during his *Hear Women Tell* interview, my heart immediately began pounding. I wasn't used to having the tables turned.

There's a sense of risk whenever you invite someone to become a part of your story or fiddle with its make u As a teller, I view my storytelling as a performance. I want it to be perfect. As Kevin and I entered into the story mediation it took a while for me to release the fear of messing u I found myself repeating his words in my head, "It's okay to play, it's okay to play, it's okay to play."

Kevin's interjections and interruptions are key to disengaging the critic in your head. He likes to surprise you with curve balls. How did that make you—the character—feel? Why did you do that? What if so and so responded differently? What did the room look like? What if something totally different happens?

In the end my experience with Kevin as a story mediator opened me up to exploring my stories in a new way. It's easy to spend so much time carefully editing, trimming, and correcting a story to fit into a tidy beginning, middle, and end—where the end is a perfectly wrapped conclusion—that it can become narrowed by your own story development process.

Playing with story mediation lets you safely explore the potential richness of the story that drew you to it in the first place. It gives you permission to take detours and blind alleys and different endings and find hidden treasure. In the process you flesh out the possible underpinnings of the story that can make it richer in the long run, even if you never use the ideas that arise during story mediation play.

The key for me was to remain present and relaxed in the story mediation experience. It's my nature to steer the process, but Kevin's story mediation disrupts that and though that can be unsettling, it also freed me of my usual methods of thinking about story. By doing so, it opened up for me the possibility of finding the best of the story.

It's like being a kid on the playground and you see yourself as a cowboy and then another kid tells you that you have to be an Indian because there are too many cowboys already. That one thing totally changes how you see yourself in the story. (Hillenburg, 2012)

Reflect about the Experience

Ask what the teller gained from the experience. This is another time to deeply listen to the teller. When you provide feedback after this, when possible, use the teller's specific words when addressing what they learned. They own this. The story mediator shares in a caring way what the teller said they learned and experienced.

In the next chapter, I will address what happens when not one person but whole groups, help create the story, using a dramatic playful practice I call *ensemble storytelling* (Cordi 2009).

If we were all determined to play the first violin we should never have an ensemble. Therefore, respect every musician in his proper place.
—Robert Schumann, German Composer

Chapter 7
Moving Play into Ensemble Storytelling

As noted, story-crafting is enriched with the addition of a story mediator who not only listens, but also enters the story with the teller. The story mediator directs and engages in different and diverse ways by working inside the story. The story mediator can also incorporate the audience into the coaching process as participants. The audience is invited to experience the story vicariously, examining and reflecting on the process. The experience is quite rewarding, often leading to thoughtful discourse.

Drawing on this method, there is another way to involve the audience and that is from playing with pedagogy I call ensemble storytelling. Ensemble storytelling is a mediated way to use play to co-author story with a small or large group. This is achieved in two ways.

Open Ensemble Storytelling

The audience can actively enter the story as story-crafter participants called upon at specific times to respond in the meditated fictional world, often becoming characters at significant points within the story. During these times, the listening audience no longer watches the story, but instead make collective story choices that help the teller see the story in a new way. This can include creating a whole new version of the story or simply helping to extend the environment. For example, the audience, now serving as ensemble participants, create sounds when entering a scary part of the forest as though they are in the woods. They become a soundtrack. This helps the teller imagine the woods as though it was occurring now. Another way that audience can be called upon to be a participant in the story is to highlight the voices in the story. They also could be called upon to become other voices in the story. For example, the story might occur at a party and in order to create the party, the audience provides the voices of party attendees. Each audience member becomes actively involved in creating the specific story or a time in the story. Each story-crafter, when called upon, can create to serve the story.

Closed Ensemble Storytelling

Closed ensemble storytelling occurs without an audience. In a closed ensemble, a group co-authors a narrative or a piece of the narrative not when called upon, but instead, during the entire story composition. From the initial idea, all group members are co-creators. No one yells, "Do you have an idea?" Instead, people are invited from the beginning to create and actually engage in their creation by stepping into the story as a group. This is pedagogy of practice used in education. It finds roots in process or educational drama, by drawing on the work of educational drama scholars like Brian Edmiston, who uses inquiry to build narratives. He refers to this practice as dramatic inquiry. He also refers to it as dialogic inquiry. Edmiston states,

> In dialogic inquiry learners collaboratively explore the meaning and co-author understanding about topics and narratives … learners make meaning about real and imagined worlds. Over time, inquiry opens up meaning to new possibilities as inquirers learn from and with one another in ongoing authentic, substantive, polyphonic, dialogic conversations focused by implicit or explicit inquiry questions. (2012 40)

Closed ensemble storytelling draws upon this inquiry-based learning. But instead of serving to teach in an educational context, it is used to co-create narratives, to influence and negotiate the work of story-making for story-crafters. The group uses a collective imagination to move the story to reenactment. Essential to making sure all voices are heard as ideas depends on the negotiation skills of the story mediator. The story mediator makes choices, which can lead to jumping in to the fictional world. This is a point when the ensemble story-crafters can enter the fiction. The key difference is that ensemble storytelling is used to create powerful narratives or to promote inquiry that will help frame the story. In educational drama, the use of process drama is to teach, but even in process drama, what is learned can be formatted into a production (O'Neill 1982).

Asking questions and then using ensemble storytelling to address the question can help story-crafters invest and engage in the story-making process. This is not to say that from this ensemble play, the desired outcome can't be rich inquiry and/or the shaping of story performance. After all, the purpose of playing with stories, with or without an ensemble group, is to find new directions in the story that the story-crafter can use in their work. As you ask questions, the story builds, but often using ensemble storytelling, so do the questions. The story serves the inquiry and the inquiry serves the many stories that are co-created from the process.

The story mediator guides participants in playful and dramatic exercises, questions, and mediation inviting engagement and discussion in the story as it occurs. It is not so much as telling a story, but investment in the fiction created. In this fictional world, each person represents a different role. However, the roles can switch to serve the narrative created. The skillful story mediator can aggregate the tension of the story or highlight a new perspective that may change the roles. The important work of the story mediator is to continue the rich choices that are made from the co-creators or should I say co-crafters of the story. A skillful story mediator negotiates how the fiction occurs but the negotiation comes to play when he or she makes sure all ideas are accepted. The guiding philosophy of "Yes, and … " (McDowell, n.d.) requires time and skill and practice.

What is essential is that the co-crafters work to serve the narrative. It is not about who tells the best story, but instead, how can the story-crafters investigate, negotiate, and even interrogate this narrative so that we can learn about it? However, together we can explore a single story episode, changing the beats to invite more tension, or we can even take on a new direction for the co-created story. This is a time for true ensemble play.

Ensemble

An ensemble is more than people gathering together to work on a single idea. With story-crafting, they serve the story using play to dig deeper into a co-created narrative.

The book, *Contemporary Ensemble: An Interview with Theatre-makers* (Radosavljević, 2013) defines ensemble as "originating from the Middle English adverb (via French and Latin) meaning 'at the same time'" (2). Ensemble storytelling is, in actuality, concerned about the story-making that occurs in synchronicity with the story mediator. From this skillful use, a story is experienced. It is not told, but felt by the dramatic play that is used by the ensemble. This all happens at the same time.

As a noun, ensemble is defined a collection of people working together; viewing the world together and not as individuals. In ensemble storytelling, the co-creators can see the story differently, but must work to serve the story. Serving the story are the choices made by each member of the ensemble to move the group to see and experience the story in innovative ways. The focus is on the needs of the narrative. The goal of ensemble work is to represent a work ethos which is collective, creative and collaborative.

> ... whether by means of individual members making the same kind of contribution (devising) or making distinct kinds of contribution toward the same artistic outcome (writing, directing, composing, designing, and performing). (12)

Ensemble work is about design, not in the creation of a final work. The design lies in the goal of the ensemble players—to intricately articulate a way to represent, understand, and engage in the fictional world. In this design, each person needs to open to each other's ideas as they orient the way the fictional world is presented.

Ensemble work is both unique and involving. Ensemble actor Joanna Holden, who has worked with Cirque du Soleil, said of her experience:

> You can almost interpret each other's ideas before the person has even thought of it. And that is a beautiful environment to be in. Very creative, very free because of the trust that has been developed between you. (110)

What makes the ensemble work is trust. This is when the story-crafters avoid creating predetermined scripts, but instead, they work from an idea or a question. From this question, build the ensemble to answer it. Trust is essential to explore the story-making process. In ensemble storytelling, the story mediator builds that trust, inviting all suggestions to be used.

The work of Improvisational Comedy and Ensemble Storytelling

Drawing from the work of improvisational comedy, story mediators use the guiding philosophy of "Yes, and ..." (McDowell). This is where the co-creators take all suggestions. Regardless of the suggestion, all choices are honored. In improv comedy, these suggestions support the game to create the most effective performance-based experience, not only for the players, but also for an anticipated audience. In ensemble storytelling, these suggestions are used to help create a shared fictional world. They are used to serve the story to benefit the tellers. Since the work is suggested in play, there is more acceptance for the ideas. For example, when working in an ensemble fashion, if a story-crafter suggests that Red's cloak is actually blue in "Little Red Riding Hood", the suggestion is accepted. It may not make sense, but in play, the sense can come later or not at all. It is in play that these risks can surface. Would it not be fun to play with the story of "Little Blue Riding Hood?" In play, all things are possible.

Improvisational comedians draw much from this philosophy, especially Second City in Chicago. Other groups, like The Annoyance Theater in Chicago and See You Thursday with the company, Columbus Unscripted in Columbus, advocate that they open up more to the idea that they don't have to be governed by rules, but by a communal sense of working together. Improvisational teams do not deny the reality that the improvisation occurs. They work with this environment and when they make a change, it is done with the intention to move the improvisation in a way that increases the depth or the risk. An improvisational comedy team works hard to take all the suggestions made by the group, but sometimes these are negated to better play in the game of the improvisation. An improvisational player works hard to heighten the improvisation, and like an improv actor, the ensemble storyteller works to accept the suggestions and avoid negating ideas.

Negation of Ideas

If a story mediator negates ideas of an ensemble company, it can result in the breaking of trust within the company. It can result in unhealthy competition of ideas to see which will be chosen by the group or mediator. Too often players are trying to outdo or win over someone. The story mediator is a skillful player, but if he or she does the work well, it is the group that accepts all of the ideas. The story mediator creates a place where this can happen. He or she can also remind others in and out of the fictional world, that in play, one can accept everything. Ensemble storytelling should be about creating a story world together.

Play invites risk taking. Not all suggestions will work, but a better ensemble is formed by the experience. Effective story mediators will accept the risks that come from moving the story in different ways because they have created an environment in which ideas are accepted by all.

For example, if an ensemble member shares that a blue giraffe has entered the story, the team accepts without question—yes—and builds on the idea that the giraffe is now in the story—and—. Even though the ideas are accepted, the story mediator determines how much power the suggestions serve for the tellers and the story.

Using Power in the Fictional World

In my work with Edmiston in 2009, he illustrated that there were three types of power when working in the fictional world. There is power over someone, power for someone, and power with someone. If an ensemble story-crafter introduces a blue giraffe in the story, the story mediator—or another ensemble player—can demonstrate power over the suggestion. "Now that we have this giraffe, we will store him in the garage." The story mediator accepts that giraffe, but quickly uses his or her power to minimize their influence in the story. Demonstration of power for someone is where the story mediator or someone else empowers the suggestion. "We have this blue giraffe and I believe we should ride it to take us to our destination. In fact, I think this giraffe will help us get there quicker and safer." Notice that the story mediator empowers the suggestion of the teller. In demonstrating power with someone, the story mediator, or someone else, can align with the suggestion. "What a great idea to bring in a blue giraffe. In fact, I will take care of feeding it every day." Notice that in this example, the story mediator aligns with the teller in shaping the story.

Using power in the fictional world is an effective tool to help empower or when called upon, to disempower a teller in the ensemble. Again, the important thing is that each choice serves the story that is being co-authored and collaboratively created. The story mediator can mediate how often or how much the blue giraffe will be integrated into the story. Here is an example of how I used power when working with a student.

> A group of fifth graders studying the book *Weasel* (1991) by Cynthia Felice used process drama to explore how to defend themselves against attackers before the colonization of America. A young boy said, in order to protect himself, "I will use my machine gun." As a story mediator, I did not deny his suggestion; I accepted the machine gun during this time even though I knew it was not possible. Instead of negating this suggestion, I lessened the power it had in our story-based drama. I informed him that we can have this thing called machine gun but we didn't have any way to understand or load it. I then asked the ensemble members if anyone knew how to fire it. No one offered the information. I said we don't have enough time to learn a new weapon and I see that it has no bullets contained in the chamber. I suggested that instead we use a musket. I didn't negate his idea, but rather de-emphasized its relevance within the co-created story.

Ensemble Storyteller Serves the Story.

The Upright Citizens Brigade (UCB), founded by Amy Poehler, Ian Roberts, Matt Walsh and Matt Besser, emphasizes finding the game as the result of improvisation. Besser refers to the game of "finding the funny" and respecting those that work to make it happen. They caution against following the plot of a story.

> *Don't follow plot*—New improvisers will often hear the note, "you ended up following the plot in that scene." We are not interested in the story of a Long Form comedy scene; we are interested in the Game. We are not creating a play with a story arc. We are not interested in finding a strong beginning, middle, or end, and we aren't improvising to discover what is going to change about our characters. We are improvising comedy sketches, not stories. (Walsh, Roberts and Besser 2013 202)

In ensemble storytelling, although we are not seeking out the game in the work, we do serve the story and sometimes by heightening the game, one discovers more of the narrative possibilities in the story. First and foremost we are working to serve the story and not always to make the audience laugh. Both improv performers and ensemble storytellers work to make the episodes real and memorable. In ensemble storytelling, the story is connected to all the choices. In improv there is more freedom to stray away from a narrative arc. Ensemble storytelling works with one story exploring its many sides. Improvisation is not concerned with the beginning, middle, or end; in fact, it can illuminate a snapshot of a fictional time. In ensemble storytelling, the story mediator is not focused on completing the story, but instead, digging deeper to reveal its strengths, weakness, and areas of concern. Because improvisational comedy searches for the game, the choices are to become better improvisational players and to work to maximize the strength of the company. In ensemble storytelling, the game and the risks can illuminate the story, but the two focal points are the teller and the tale. During ensemble storytelling, the audience is involved and incorporated into the work. There is no external audience.

We are not putting on a show, but instead playing so as to be better informed about the tale. This play is about improvising stories and not creating sketch comedies. However, each art form can learn from another. Storytellers should be involved in improvisational comedy teams to find new ways to work together. Improvisational comedy teams can also learn from ensemble storytellers. Story-crafters need to involve themselves in all the arts that are aligned with narrative construction. Improvisational comedians are skilled in creating narratives from an impulse; they have much to teach the story-crafter.

The story-crafter's goals align with Bonczek and Storck's *Ensemble Story-making* (2013).

> They collaborate. As ensemble leader, you must collaborate
> with your ensemble, not dictate to it. You're not relinquishing
> your authority or allowing a non-unifying vision; there is
> plenty of room to collaborate without yielding your leadership
> Encourage your group to collaborate in the process. Let them
> have a voice. (18)

Bonczek and Storck also outline the three reasons why ensembles do not succeed:

1. One or more members lack commitment, sacrifice, and/or support, resulting in no trust, no bond.
2. The leader doesn't allow members adequate collaboration.
3. The leader allows the collaborative spirit to overrun proceedings and doesn't keep things on track. (18)

Ensemble storytelling works when everyone serves the story. However, the story does not consist of a beginning, middle, or end. It can come from a story spark or an idea, or simply a sound. What is important is that everyone works together to dig deeper and become reflective in the exploration of the story. The story or story idea is not simply discussed, but instead created by the ensemble. This is fruitful work and only becomes better with time and continual reflection. Take the time with your ensemble story-crafters and start in small intervals of time. Take fifteen minutes and reflect on what happens afterwards. Build as a company so one creates trusts and support. You will be surprised by the results.

Two Kinds of Ensemble Storytelling

As mentioned there are two primary ways that ensemble storytelling can be used to help develop story-making work. Open ensemble storytelling is a method by which the story mediator calls on the audience at specific times to change their role from audience to participants. Under the story mediator's instructions, in some way, the participants enter the story for the purpose of serving the story and the teller.

Closed ensemble storytelling occurs when a teller or a whole group decides to explore a question or idea by co-authoring a story together from the beginning to the end of the experience. There is no external audience. The audience serves only the participatory role. They offer suggestions, which the story mediator uses to enact a story-based drama. The drama is used to help the teller's trouble, and understand, or question the tale that emerges from the drama.

Below I have explored the steps to make both methods successful for story-crafters.

Open Ensemble Storytelling

In this method, the story mediator will select times that the audience will not serve in a listening role, but instead become participants in the story that is being told.

Start with an invitation The story mediator invites the audience to engage in oral exercises to help the teller know more about the story. In any given moment, they can be asked to enter the story in order to serve the teller and/or story. The audience works to authentically represent the requests of the mediator. The story mediator explains that their participation is not part of a show, but instead a *showing*, a visual display of how the story might look as a result of the mediation.

The mediator asks questions and finds a place to jump in the story. The mediator and the tellers discover the story together. But before they can do this, the story mediator asks questions to help learn more about the story. The questions asked are used to paint a picture of the story, which could include backstories waiting to be told. The audience deeply listens to the story and will soon be asked to further invest in the story. The audience helps clarify points as well. For example, when a teller shares a story about a roller coaster that falls apart when he or she was riding it, an audience member's background may help to understand the problem. He may have worked on roller coasters for six years and could share why they break down to help elevate the story. This can help the teller with the tale he or she is composing. The story mediator keeps the focus on the teller and the story and is careful not to listen to all the broken roller coaster stories, but to keep directing the focus back to the sections that will help build the story.

I recently worked with Simon Brooks, a British Storyteller who lives in New England. He is an accomplished teller and voice-over artist. I asked him to talk about his experience during his story mediation with me. I asked Simon questions to help me know more about the story but also to learn more about the story. I also wanted my questions to be playful so he knew that we would engage in playful work. I asked him to tell me more about the story. I have included some of his comments. Simon said of the experience:

> When I began telling my story, Kevin would offer comments, or ask questions about the characters and story and I had to respond from inside the story. At first this was a little

disconcerting, but Kevin eased me into the process. When I shook that feeling off, and allowed myself to be in the story and responding to Kevin's input, I found myself led in directions I had not contemplated. He moved on to ask my character's name, does the character like tea, how the character feels, speak, etc. while requiring me to stay in the story. (Brooks 2013)

The mediator and the teller jump into the story together. The audience is in cue to join in when asked. There is a point during the questioning when the mediator finds a place to jump into the story. The story mediator finds a place to move the question and/or response to become an invite to join in the fictional world of the story. Although the mediator keeps the story flowing, there are many times when the audience can assist and the story mediator will invite them to do so. For example, as the mediator, I worked with a woman who engaged in a story about playing under a radioactive fence in Las Alamos, New Mexico. For some reason, the teller did not recognize the possibility of harm in the fence, so I needed to mediate with the teller to discuss and see the fence. I quietly signaled the audience to make the sounds of the fence as she told the story. Side coaching her, I informed her to keep telling, but listen to the noise. This focused her attention on the fence. With a wave of my hand, the audience slowly encircled her as though they were the fences. She closed her eyes to concentrate more on the tension of the tale and opened her eyes to find a human fence surrounding her. This experience made it more real; she remembered back to the actual fence recalling more and more details from the sounds and actions of the participants. In the story mediation, I wanted her to see and engage with the fence. At one point, she heard less of my side coaching and told me about the impact of the fence.

A successful story mediator should disappear as the story moves to the forefront. The audience—as active story participants—will help foreground the story. The audience can help this arrive quicker. The story mediator uses audience members as participants to help the teller envision what he or she reveals. In order to do this, the story mediator listens to the teller discuss the story and finds ways to move the audience into the story. There are many ways to involve the audience as participants. Some of them include:

1. *Create a soundscape.* The audience becomes the sound of the story as the teller shares the work. For example, a teller spoke of

an old ship traveling across the water and with a simple gesture from me as story mediator, the audience made ocean sounds, bird calls, created waves, and began real conversation that might have occurred on the ship. Every story has its own soundtrack. Hearing it inspires the teller to envision and engage in the story.

2. *Reveal a silent character.* A teller might benefit from having an audience member stand in as though he or she is a person in the story. As a mediator, I often ask the teller to address the person as though he is a character. The character says nothing but the physical presence is enough for the teller to give direction to his or her talk or thoughts.

3. *Become a vocal character.* Invite an audience to enter a conversation with you as a specific character. In the case of Simon's mediation, I had him verbally pen a love letter as someone stood in and eventually addressed him. Simon describes his experience below.

The tale was a love story from one of the Scandinavian sagas, where the protagonist is a craftsman and the lover is a swan maiden/Valkyrie. Kevin asked me to write—tell—a love letter to my Valkyrie explaining why I wanted my true love back. This was no small feat to come up with something on the spot, but it made me look at the protagonist's motives. This was all done in the moment with almost no time to think.

… Kevin quietly pulled someone from the group/audience and had him or her play the lover, as it were, responding to the love letter I was reciting. Kevin asked for a better letter from me and again for a response from my love. Kevin then threw a complete curve ball and asked each other member of the group a question relating to a certain part or character from the story. He asked one person to portray the craft that I was willing to give up for my love—as I had said in my letter— and they said that so many people need my craft, and that my lover is just one woman and I should let her go. Another person was asked to be the Valkyrie's sister and to address the Valkyrie. The response was, "Why should my sister leave our family, the gods, to be with him—what had he done for her?" Another audience member was asked to be a blind person for whom I had made shoes—"I feel like I can fly when I wear your shoes"—another was the Valkyrie's father to address

my lover—"Do what you want I want nothing to do with
you anymore."—The latter was a very powerful statement.

4. *Strengthen a stronger voice using the teller's dialogue.* The
   audience can echo the dialogue of the teller. There are certain
   points when the listeners can rhythmically echo back the
   words of the character or an action. This can help place a
   deeper focus on the words and often the teller will revisit the
   impact of the words.

5. *Illustrate possible ways to address tension.* Audience members
   can show, in a dramatic way, alternative ways to deal with
   tension. For example, in order to study the character of
   King Arthur, they might explore what happens when Merlin
   denies his request for help. In duet or small groups, each
   audience member show reactions that may not be in the
   story but can be displayed.

6. *Demonstrate possible ending or beginning choices.* The
   audience members can be used to help explore the teller's
   choices for beginning and ending a story. Remember , play
   works in the possible and the impossible. Seeing alternative
   methods can help the teller to envision the story differently
   than the pre-planned way they have designed.

7. *Create a tableau.* In a tableau, participants make still images
   with their bodies to represent a scene. A tableau can be used
   to quickly establish a scene that involves a large number
   of characters. Because there is no movement, a tableau is
   easier to manage than a whole-group improvisation – yet
   it can easily lead into extended drama activities. It can be
   used to explore a particular moment in a story or drama,
   or to replicate a photograph or artwork for deeper analysis.
   (dramaresource.com 2014)

8. *Become the words a character is thinking or not thinking.*
   A group makes a still image and individuals are invited to
   speak their thoughts or feelings aloud—just a few words. This
   can be done by tapping people on the shoulder or holding
   a cardboard *thought-bubble* above their head. Alternatively,
   thought tracking (also called *thought tapping*) can involve
   other members of the class speaking one character's thoughts
   aloud for them. (dramaresource.com 2014)

React in a different genre or form. The story mediator connects to the story by asking the teller to place it in a different form. An example would be that I asked Simon to create a love letter. This is a new genre—love letter—and a new form—writing.

9. *Narrator role*—An audience can be the voice, like the movie trailer voice that explains the film. However, in this case, the person narrates certain scenes of the story.

10. *Hot seat interviews*—This strategy is derived from a theater technique called *hot-seating*, where characters are interviewed about their background, behavior and motivation. (dramaresource.com 2014)

11. *Overhead conversations*—Using *choral speak*, the audience conveys some of the story as though it were gossip or town talk. "Did you hear about …?" "I heard …"

12. *Alter-ego*—This is where a member of the audience acts or becomes the person that the character would never be—the opposite character.

13. *Demonstrate flashback of an episode*—Audience members can show past scenes be enacting them for the teller to witness.

14. *Re-enactment*—Audience members can help the teller re-envision the scene by reenacting it for the teller and story mediator.

Simon Brooks Describes the Process

The important thing to remember is that the story mediator carefully selects how these techniques can be used to serve the teller and the story. There is no systematic order, but instead the story mediator uses these techniques to build perspective or reflection. It is important to understand the process. Simon shares more about the process of working with an invisible mediator:

> During this process Kevin became invisible even though he was asking for all this input from many different people—there were 15 of us. He guided us through this process carefully and with compassion. He was quiet, yet firm, asking

for more and more; yet it felt as if he were not there, other than as a shadow or ghost/spirit. We stayed within the story—and this is important—whilst he stayed outside, directing us through the mediation. The responses and actions of the other participants were embedded in the story through this play. With Kevin's mediation, or direction of the others, and by keeping everyone within the story this, for me, became a very visceral experience. (Brooks 2013)

Please note that as a story mediator my job is to appear like the shadow that Simon speaks. However, at all times I am in and out of the fictional world. I often will step out of the shadow and become a player or director of the fictional world.

On expanding the story choices—This process opened up so many real choices and voices to listen to in the story, not only those within it, but also those external to the story. These were voices and choices that I could never have come up with on my own, because they came from other people who think in their own ways. Because these participants brought their own life experiences to the work, it opened up places I could rarely, possibly never, have found on my own. These motives and viewpoints … brought a whole new depth to the work. The process left me thinking: Why is this story so important for me to tell? Where does it come from? What can I now bring to the story that I was not able to before? I have asked myself the first two questions, but prior to this work, have not answered with such depth and meaning.

On the uniqueness of this work—Although I have done workshops in which I have explored motives of characters before, or imagined myself in the story's environment and culture before, this was a very different experience. Those workshops have been great and I have learned a great deal from them. I have also done work on my own with play, and through research, to get within the story to find where it comes from—not just culturally—and where I want to take it, what voice to tell the tale in, and what I can bring to a story. The experience with this new process is so rich, deep and, most of all, so dynamic, using group work. I think this is the key to it—the group dynamic, carefully mediated, allowing the storyteller to see and hear very different perspectives and worldview points from others. (2013)

My last point, if it can be called that, is that I want this method of working to be the norm for me. Group working or coaching is, I believe, the way of the future, the new method by which to learn. Well, maybe not learn, but rather we need to know the stories first. We need to know that before we reach this point, to tackle it this way, to use this process. I think for me, knowing a story first, and then bringing the story within the play dynamic that this process uses, will bring a richness and depth, even quality, to a tale that cannot be reached in any other way.

I saw the experience as playing with a matryoshka doll. I had been looking at the painting and details on the outside of the first doll—the story—but Kevin's work revealed there are many other dolls inside waiting to be explored and acknowledged—the places and characters, including those not in the story when it is told. Other workshops have had me look at some—but not all—of these dolls individually, but not share them with others, and then play with all the dolls together with everyone. There are some stories—"Goldilocks" for example—which do not need this much depth or amount of deep work. There are, however, a great many other stories that could not only benefit from this sort of work, but should be required to go through this process, to allow, or bring, such depth and meaning to a story. (Brooks 2013)

For more of Simon's work, go to http://www.diamondscree.com.

Closed Ensemble Storytelling—There is No External Audience

All members co-create the story with the guidance of the story mediator.

Ensemble storytelling for performance—Storytellers often work alone, but what happens when whole groups co-author and co-create a story for performance? This has been a practice I have been involved as teller and story mediator for the past twenty years. I was recently in New York, working with the old folktale *The Talkative Turtle,* with over thirty students from first through eighth grade. I started with what Elder Vi Hilbert referred to as the skeleton of the tale. This is literally a thirty-second sharing of the essential bones of the tale. After telling this, I asked the students to provide the flesh of the story. Soon ideas abounded. Every idea was used to co-create the story. However,

I often take these suggestions while the students are in the story. I side coach out suggestions and in role, they might recommend possible directions. Soon ideas were introduced, such as strapping the turtle to a rocket to help him fly or building the Space Shuttle and strapping the turtle to it. We used play to co-create and perform the story. I used many of the story mediation tools and in under an hour, we performed this story for over four hundred and fifty students and teachers. However, what made this work was the fact that, as story mediator, I continued to make sure we were telling the narrative together. This included having single character play out in choral fashion. So instead of one turtle, we had fifteen. We employed many of the suggestions mentioned above including thought tracking and tableaux. As the story mediator we co-create and use all suggestions to build the narrative.

Another time, I worked with forty youth and adults to explore the tale, "The Ghost of One Black Eye". The frame of the story was set, but we negotiated all the suggestions to create a stronger story than the skeleton that I shared with them. When the story is told, it simply mentions that a mother and father have a big family. However, negotiating the story with the group, the big family took shape. Soon, the father purchased a home for his thirty-eight children. A *Star Wars*-loving kid wanted to take a light saber so we had twelve light sabers with which to confront the monster, but they still ended up running away as the bare bones strategy suggests. The monster was brighter than the light saber, and as a story mediator, I made the choice to empower the monster, not the sword. I often used the kids to echo the language. "I am the ghost of one black eye." In performance, we had over five hundred people chant this with the students. This definitely empowered the tellers on stage. Ensemble storytelling can break the rules of the tale. Instead of a small family in a large house, I extended it to be over forty people in a mansion. This helps to invite the ensemble nature of the tale. In ensemble storytelling for performance, the story mediator can work with a whole group finding parts of the story where all can be involved. I needed to honor the development of the story, but we continued to negotiate the way we arrived at the conclusion.

Choosing ensemble tales—When I search for ensemble stories I look for ones that we can adapt and ones for which we can include many tellers. I look for a story that is open to co-creation. Rhymed tales like *The Cat in the Hat* depend on specific language and are not as workable but a tale like the ghost tale "Tailey Bone" can invite more to the story. We can have numerous people visit the old man and why not have fifteen dogs instead of three? I also cocreate stories simply from an idea such as, "Did the giant from 'Jack and the Beanstalk' have a brother, and if he did, what would he be doing now?" We begin wrestling with this question and building a story from the multiple ideas and responses. Whole performances can be created from an ensemble's suggestions. However, they must be able to use play to try them out. They need mediation so they don't become stuck to one idea.

Some of you are probably asking, how is that possible? Although I have often served to tell the story with kids, the key in this work, is that I was serving more of the role of mediator than teller. I let the students and/or adults take ownership of the tale. The ideas that they shared, we used, but I served to help transition them into the story. Saying this, I did mediate it to make sure that the story was heard and experienced. In this chapter, I have outlined the steps that I have taken to make this work.

Ensemble storytelling for inquiry—Story-crafters leave unresolved issues or questions alive in their stories. Imagine, instead of retreating to a quiet desk to wrestle with possible written solutions, inviting fifteen story-crafters to imagine and engage sections of the story as an ensemble. The story mediator leads the discovery process, addressing an unresolved issue or beginning a story from a frame and asking basic questions to drive their thoughts.

In working with a school, I decided to explore an unresolved issue in a classic tale. Instead of retelling "The Three Little Pigs" with elementary students, we examined the story's dramatic structure asking the students to consider what happened to the pigs? The story was now set in a new frame—homicide crime scene—where students transformed into experts who wanted to know more about how the pigs had been killed or where they were killed. We had one fallen pig, but did not where the rest were. In no time at all, using teacher or storyteller-in-role, students searched as forensics investigators to discover how the pigs had or had not died. They asked, "What did the suspect look like?" "Where did this bloodstain come from?" The students created the bloodstain, negotiating the fiction they were creating together. "What is this piece of chinny chin?" We even drew a chalk outline of the dead pig to develop our understanding. Instead of letting the story's plot direct our inquiry, we improvised. Heathcote notes,

> Improvisation ... means discovering by trial, error, and testing; using available materials with respect for their nature, and being guided by the appreciation of their potential. The end product of improvisation is the *experience* of it. (1984 45)

We introduced and instigated trouble, changing the intensity of the episodes, and using role, we dug deep into the unresolved questions in the class: Three Little Pigs. Some would say this would work better with younger kids, but the same techniques were employed when I worked with teenagers. With teens and adults in Cleveland, using fictional play, we explored why the Titanic had sunk. At one point, I was in charge of guarding the engineers from the press; another time I played a passenger who had survived; still another time I became a clergyman who was trying to console Captain John Smith. The world we co-created often called for me to be in role and respond in role to questions students asked. When in role, I am able to assume characters in a story, increase narrative tensions, and make the story richer, deeper, and more meaningful. These types of experiences can also be employed in story-crafting circles.

Spotlight on Story Mediation and Ensemble Storytelling in Missouri

One of the best ways to understand this process is to hear how others were involved in story mediation and ensemble work. This is a personal account from Flavia Everman, a storyteller from Missouri. She has been featured at the St. Louis Storytelling Festival and recently had the opportunity to collect stories from Rwanda. In our story mediation we worked with a popular folktale that she had just discovered. She first discussed my questioning of the story.

> I really appreciated your take on interrupting our story to ask questions. I often do this when I'm directing a play and I think it drives the actors crazy, but I want them to "feel" the words, not just recite them. I think that is what you wanted us to do that evening, "feel" the story instead of just reciting it. (2011)

Then we see her work with a story in progress.

> I wanted to try something completely new for this workshop, and I had just recently read "Sody Sallyratus" that day. I

wanted to start from scratch without any preconceived actions or bad habits. We sat together and as I started the story, you questioned me about the environment, the personalities of the main characters, what they were wearing, and what did the house look like. It really brought home the entire scene in my mind. I saw the people, the home in the Appalachians, and the surrounding woods.

As I went along in the story, you played with being different characters and we proceeded to hold conversations, ad libbing as we went. The audience asked about suggestions for different voices, characteristics for the bear and such. We bounced off of each other's characters and the story went quickly. That is the beauty of story mediation—a story can morph in ways that no one foresees, creating a masterpiece with all new creative juices. (Everman 2011)

Even though it has been three years since I coached—mediated—her, I asked her via email to dig deeper into the experience. This is what she shared. As one can see she quickly begins to visualize and actualize the narrative

When we first started, you asked what the characters were wearing. Since this story was rooted in the Appalachians, I pictured the mom in a light blue dress with an apron, checking the cupboards meticulously in case someone had moved the baking soda. How was she supposed to make those golden brown biscuits without baking soda? You asked about the biscuits and as I bake, I described the biscuits being golden brown, raised to perfection, steam coming off of them and when broken open, a pad of butter melting into the delicious flaky texture of the soft white insides of the biscuit. (2011)

In my mediation I noticed that what was critical was the desire for the baking soda, so I changed the work to address this.

The story seemed to then revolve around the need for the baking soda and the family's desire for these tasty treats. The boy could be seen with rolled up pants and maybe a slingshot in his hip pocket. The husband was just a laid back sort of character who didn't get riled up easily. The wife, however, seemed to get more and more agitated as the story went along, as her family didn't seem to be nearly as concerned over the biscuits as she was. This culminated in a conversation between herself—me—and her husband—you—with her tapping her fingers and him answering simply until she finally pestered him out the door to find the children and that necessary baking soda. (Everman 2011)

We did not plan for the squirrel to be a dominant character but he was.

As the story progressed, conversations ensued between the shop owner and each character. You would switch between characters, forcing me to develop personalities for each character. You would start a character's personality and I would build it from there and vice versa. At one time, the shopkeeper was very nonchalant about the missing characters and not very vocal at all, mostly saying "Yup" or "Nope" when asked. This dialogue was extremely useful as I never knew what you were going to say and what reactions your character was going to have. I had to play off of the verbiage and make the story flow where I wanted it to go, including your newly-introduced perspective and personalities. This was like taking a photograph and really looking at the background of the picture, noticing the kinds of trees, the mannerisms of the characters, the colors of the flowers, the flow of the stream, the length of the bridge, and the items in the shop. (2011)

At this point I used open ensemble storytelling to invite the audience to help us understand the bear.

When we came to the bear, *if* you stopped the story and asked the audience about what a bear would look like, what would it sound like. The audience brought in different suggestions, asking "what kind of bear?" "How big is it?" ""What sound would it make? I then used this information to make my arms wide to show that it was a big bear and said in the lowest voice I could, "Ah, a little boy ... looks like lunch to me! And some Soddy Sallyratus too." I then caught up the boy in my arms and made my mouth as big as it would go and leaned my head back and "swallowed" that little boy. As each character came by, I made provisions according to the size of each person. This really helped me to see the bear and actually incorporate a personality with him. The squirrel was similar as he was a fidgety creature and I made quick movements for him and talked in a fast, squeaky voice. These actions came from suggestions from the audience as well. (Everman 2011)

Flavia makes some final comments on the work.

This type of coaching—story mediation—really brings a new depth to stories and asks questions, creating different perspectives for each story. This type of coaching can be used over and over on the same story, emphasizing different aspects of the story and changing it to follow that line of questioning. There really is so much to see in the words of a story. (2011)

With ensemble storytelling, story-crafters, writers, teachers, and other imaginative thinkers, are not tied to a written text or a determined plot. They play with the ideas as an ensemble. Many concerted voices, enhanced by story mediation, can move rich narratives to become richer and story ideas to become full stories.

Invite a community of practice that engages and plays with stories. The next chapter explores how to make this practice consistent, increasing play to become part of a rich imaginative community of story-crafters. The next chapter will talk about the need to play by creating communities of practice.

Without this playing with fantasy no creative work has ever yet come to birth. The debt we owe to the play of imagination is incalculable.
—Carl Gustav Jung, Swiss Psychiatrist

Chapter 8
Establishing a Story-Crafting Community that Invites Play

As story-crafters, we need community. This means that we need consistency in time and place in which to share our work together. It is true that we often practice alone, but this does not have to be. Instead, I would like to issue a call for us to play and work together. However, the play that we do as a community is not something that we should do half-heartedly or periodically, but instead with conviction and on a consistent schedule. As we have seen in this book, play is the strongest work we can do to develop our craft. We need to create a community where play is accepted, welcomed, and part of our practice. We can only do this by sharing our methods, promises, and challenges with other story-crafters. As Gandhi states, "The best way to find yourself is to lose yourself in the service of others."

Story-crafting is a service. We write, tell, and perform for others. Few of us would be a story-crafter if no one heard or read the work. We seek the attention of an audience. However, we also need to provide a service to teach and guide and I would say mediate others to learn the craft. As the Dutch proverb reminds us, "good company makes short miles."

As story-crafters, imagine how much can we can learn when we create collaborative and co-authored communities. Too often our practice is our performance. People view us when we are ready. I caution against this as the mindset. Instead, let us collectively share our work with small groups and the larger community.

We need to not only learn from organizations dedicated to storytelling such as the National Storytelling Network—www.storynet.org—or the International Storytelling Center—www.storytellingcenter.net—but also learn about the stellar work in storytelling occurring in England with The Society for Storytelling—http://www.sfs.org.uk—or the Scottish Storytelling Centre at http://www.scottishstorytellingcentre.co.uk or the work at the International Storytelling Festival in Singapore—http://sisf.bookcouncil .sg/2013/, or countless other narrative connections. However, as story-crafters we should also reach out and attend story slams, theatre performances, rap gigs, writing conferences, and more. We need to learn how others play with story development. We need to honor the work that we know, but remain open to change based on our associations with and direct observations of how others use the arts.

A Need for Community

When I was teaching high school in California, a fifth grade boy contacted me to help him create his own youth storytelling group in his home state of Texas. He explained that he and his friends had been holding weekly meetings in the school library, performing in shows every other month. As he talked, I could feel his energy and passion for learning more about story. Even though I helped him contact the Texas guild and even called some well-known Texas tellers to assist, this student had done more to build a storytelling community than some storytelling or writing guilds I have experienced over the years.

This made me think. If this young person can organize in this way, why can't we locally, nationally, or globally? Could it be because many of us work in isolated pockets and the times we spend to share our craft is only to perform? We can take note of this young man who reached out not only to me but also to his friends and formed a group on his own. If we want to establish a community to engage in playful practice as story-crafters, why not begin with inviting a few friends to join in? Call two or three people and meet once or twice a week for the sole purpose of play. Engage in this serious work to improve the art.

The Need for Story

There are people who encounter story and don't know it is okay to study it or enjoy it. As story-crafters, we need to help offset the impression that storytelling and story sharing is relegated only to children. Children-based storytelling is powerful and rewarding, but children are not the only audiences that need narrative.

After watching my animated show at an outdoor storytelling event, a fifty-year-old woman sidled up to me with a whisper and said, "I never heard stories when I was little. Is it okay to want to hear them now?" I was stunned both that this woman needed permission for her interest and that she was raised without stories. This made me think that if storytellers were better organized as a community, and if a bigger part of our goal was to raise awareness of the art and practice of story, this might not have happened.

I think of my own story. When I was eighteen, I was awestruck at the Once Upon a Time storytelling festival at Kent State University; hearing Irish teller Bat Burns spin words and Appalachian clog dancer Rebecca Hill tell of the mountains where my parents were raised. I was a reporter for the school paper, and even though I was scheduled to attend this event for five minutes, I stayed the whole week. As a kid we only traveled to West Virginia for this one week but I traveled to mythic places, homes, and fantasy lands while remaining in my seat. However, it was not so much the journey. It was the fact that I was inside the story each person told. Each person shared a narrative and in a short time came together as story-crafters. I remember the tissues that had to be shared when we heard the cancer story and the laughter that was evoked on the first date stories. This community and their willingness to share with us transfixed me. Even though everyone was so much older than me—forties, fifties, sixties—after a week I felt connected to the community. Strangers united through story.

Although raised on West Virginia stories, I never saw myself as a teller. With this community however, I was immediately welcomed as a one, but then the conference ended. I wanted to continue to be a storyteller and the community was no longer there. As much as I felt the joy of being together, I felt the loss of letting go of what I had found. I was hooked, but I didn't have any ideas as to how to find stories or story-crafters.

Hooked on story, I aimlessly searched at my library to find old cassette tapes of Jackie Torrance, The Folktellers, Jay O'Callahan, Donald Davis, and Elizabeth Ellis. None of the tapes had images, just a library seal in clear plastic.

I wore them out practicing these tales. I felt lost and alone. Although I enjoyed the tapes, it was not enough to feed my desire to tell stories and learn in a storytelling community. My college friends did not understand my need to share folktales or personal accounts in a public way.

I found a storytelling community about a year and a half later. Driving ninety minutes each month, I met with what was then The Cleveland Storytelling Guild, now called WRAPPS. It was a great relief to find a community, but I will never forget how frustrating it was to try to learn to tell alone and rarely meet someone my own age telling stories. This is a feeling that has never left me. There are still people that feel this way and knowing this has only increased my drive to build more communities of shared story-crafting. Imagine how many people we could attract to the art of story development if we established consistent story spaces where they could learn and practice the art.

Establishing Communities of Practice

Communities of play invite reflection of the storytelling process in all of its stages. Experienced and beginning tellers need to make a mindful commitment to tell stories as they gather. They need to talk, argue constructively, take risks, and most of all, play. Cultural anthropologists Jave Lave and Etienne Wenger (1991) believe we need to be involved in learning as "communities of practice." (29). Put simply, communities must practice what they study. On the website, wenger-trayner.com, Wenger states, "Communities of practice are formed by people who engage in a process of collective learning in a shared domain of human endeavor."

The key word is practice. The work of the story-crafter needs to be reflexive, critical, and insightful. The only way this happens is if communities gather to support this as a goal. They must be advocates for story-crafting. Here are some places where story-crafting can be found.

In Schools—First of all, schools need to recognize that writing and speaking work together. When the National Council of Teachers of English (NCTE) states its position on storytelling, the framers outline the use of story. They state:

> Listeners encounter both familiar and new language patterns through story. They learn new words or new contexts for already familiar words. Those who regularly hear stories

subconsciously acquire familiarity with narrative patterns and begin to predict upcoming events. Both beginning and experienced readers call on their understanding of patterns as they tackle unfamiliar texts. Then they recreate those patterns in both oral and written compositions. Learners who regularly tell stories become aware of how an audience affects a telling, and they carry that awareness into their writing. (NCTE 1992)

NCTE develops both language and literacy. In the standard classroom, writing is viewed as a solitary, quiet act. By using play, narrative writing and telling can be positioned in a more public way. Students and teachers need a playground in which to experiment with new ideas as they write. Talking out loud before writing builds collaboration with both writing and discovering new ideas. To make this space, teachers and students should orally play with ideas to create quality writing. Consequently, playing with stories creates a public, playful act. In *Writers at Play*, Adler agrees:

> The writer, who needs freedom—air—to breathe in possibility, also needs a space in which to breathe the air. Though these imaginary worlds invite play and exploration, the work of creating and maintaining them can be quite serious (2009 4).

Why do we send students to solitary desks to brainstorm or write a first draft when they could orally play with ideas with other classmates? In addition, why not invite the teacher to mediate the play with the stories that students create? Stories come to life charged by the ideas of their classmates and the focused direction of the teacher serving as mediator.

Add oral storytelling and story-making circles to complement writing ideas. These can also be formed to create a safe space to share ideas. Imagine the rich play the teacher can incorporate when they focus on more classroom talk and stories in the classroom. Students can discuss story development and actively use play to explore their choices, instead of passively turning in an assignment and waiting for a grade. A few written comments may be less motivating than an engaged classroom experiencing and exchanging ideas.

Consider building a youth storytelling club or troupe. Judy Sima and I have written a book on this subject called *Raising Voices: Creating Youth Storytelling Groups and Troupes* (2003). In this book we outline how to build a successful storytelling community by extending learning and forming a club or troupe. Schools need to embrace narrative outreach and bring in storytelling to help align curriculum. Most of all, they need to provide students and teachers a play to rehearse and practice lessons. There is no better way than allowing students and teachers to play with their ideas.

In Writing Groups—Writing groups don't have to be a place where you only share written, completed stories. If one employs playful oral exercises, writing groups can become playgrounds for ideas. Writers can wrestle with characters orally as they share simple ideas that others help them to see, envision, or enact. Using play, the writer can explore hidden tensions by having two or three people create frozen tableaux of a scene. Oral exercises can build better and more effective writing. If writers orally talk out their ideas, they can watch the words dance, not on page but in conversation. Writers don't have to wait to discuss their work until it is a finished paper. They can orally discuss it any time. They can invite dialogue as they discuss and play out the story they want to tell and other writers can join in the work as an ensemble as they create the fiction they made together. When writing communities recognize the rich value of oral discourse and skillful play, the writing community will improve.

I must admit, I thought writing programs talked out their ideas more. However, this is not the case in many writing circles and programs. I coached—mediated—a recent graduate in the creative writing program at Ohio State University. We explored her story in depth using play. When I invited her to use these techniques in her writing circles, her response alarmed me. "We hardly ever discuss the ideas orally, we never use play." Instead, they read others' written comments and feedback only with finished drafts from which they revise. This is certainly valuable, but absent is the collaborative play. You can listen to this mediation session at www.permission2play.com Play helps build reflection and direction. Students in writing programs need to talk about their ideas as much as write them.

As a writer, I need to play more. My wish is that writing communities will be more open to the ways in which oral and written work complement each other, since both serve to create a better story.

In Storytelling Guilds—Storytelling guilds need to transition from meeting only to perform stories to interactively becoming rich playgrounds where tellers can explore ideas and work on unfinished work. A place where a storyteller can say, "I am working on this; can someone help play with this idea?" When this happens, storytelling guilds become playful labs where people partner or work as a whole group to dramatize their stories.

This is not to say that a guild should not be the place to perform; it should, but it should also be a place to work on new ideas. Where else can storytellers take risks in their work?

In Community—Entertaining is not the only reason to invite storytelling and story-making practices into your community. It can be used to dig deep into questions that community members want to explore. Storyteller Syd Lieberman was commissioned by the town of Johnstown to tell the story of the flood. Storyteller Judith Black is currently being commissioned to tell the past story of a town as a way of reviving interest in the community. This year I will travel to Qatar to help teens from the United States and Qatar to understand the region and the value that story has, not only to teach about the country, but also the relationships and changes that occur in the country. Most importantly, story is being used to voice community needs. The community officials recognized that story was a way of teaching. By employing story mediation and ensemble storytelling, questions cannot only be addressed, but be experienced. Imagine sharing a city's history by creating a story-based drama chronicling the tale? Story is a vehicle with which to share the voice.

A Call to Come Together

We need to build a practice of playing with stories. In our schools, our children learn to dig deeper by stepping into the world they are studying. In writing and storytelling guilds, more reflection and enactment can occur, thus building better communities. And in communities, story-based inquiry can address and voice the needs and desires of the people.

Imagine

Imagine a place where story-crafters are not alone in their work. A place where they dance with their words and in that dance, invite company. Using play, they watch their stories fly and scatter to places that they never knew they could. Imagine an ensemble of deep listeners that not only praise the journey of their story, but how the story-crafter told it. Imagine that a whole group of story-crafters come together and using play, live in that fictional world so the teller experiences it in a way that only play can deliver.

Now imagine … communities where play happens as a practice on a consistent basis. Places where story-crafters, risk, dream, vocalize, actualize, and play without judgment. Places where story-crafters can realize that this is their designated time to explore and discover and play. After all, in play, all things are possible.

Last but not least, I want to invite you to my efforts to build a playful community for story-crafters. Drawing from the ideas of this book, I have created the website www.permission2play.com where we will share ideas about the serious work of playing with stories. Share your story. Tell us about the promises and challenges in your journey. You can also find out new developments in this work and future work and read a continual blog addressing not only my work, but also the powerful work of other people who use play in the crafting of their stories. I would love to hear your story or address your inquiry. In this way, we are creating a collaborative community. You can also learn about organizations that foster story-crafting, play, drama, and so much more.

This is a call to come together. Let us not always do this powerful and meaningful work alone. Instead, let us play together and share our ideas. From this, new direction will come to our story-crafting. Open the door, let go of assumptions, and come ready to learn.

Drop me a line, let me know about your work and your playful adventures. Remember play is a powerful way to build a new community. You have the right to play. You have the power to change your story-crafting by taking steps to invite spoken play into your work. Invite others to come with you. It begins with you. There is no better time than now to play. Once you begin, you will not look back. The world is your playground.

Permission 2 Play Pledge
© *Kevin D. Cordi*

I give myself permission

To have fun.
To take risks.
To make mistakes.
To Play
With my thinking
my choices
my direction and development

to suspend
what I know
so
I know more

I give myself
Permission
To
fail, succeed, and play again.

I have the right to shape
My stories.

I am the crafter and creator.
I am imaginative and supportive

I know through
Play
We understand our stories
And our stories become
alive.

I give myself
Permission to Play.

About the Author

According to the National Storytelling Network, Dr. Kevin Cordi has made it his personal crusade to share the rich value of story-making and storytelling. For over twenty-seven years, he has told in over forty states, England, Japan, Scotland, Canada, and most recently Qatar. He has presented and told stories for over a million adults, children,and young adults.

He is a leading advocate for youth storytelling. He has fostered this cause by serving, among other roles, as the Executive Director for the National Youth Storytelling Olympics, now National Youth Storytelling Showcase. He created Voices Across the World Youth Storytelling Project where he registered over eighty-three youth storytelling groups in the United States, Japan, and Canada. He authored, with storyteller Judy Sima, the award-winning text *Raising Voices: Creating Youth Storytelling Groups and Troupes* For eleven years he coached, or as he would say—mediated—the award-winning youth storytelling group Voices of Illusion.

He believes that when it comes to education, one must turn to story. He holds a MA from the University of Akron, with work at East Tennessee State University in "Using storytelling as a primary means of teaching." He taught in three high schools in Ohio and California. He served, according to the National Storytelling Network, as "the first full time high school storytelling teacher in the country." He advanced his knowledge of story curriculum and furthered his work in play by securing a Ph.D. in "Storytelling and Story Making" examining the juxtaposition of dramatic play and narrative building at Ohio State University.

He now extends this work as he works with businesses, corporations, and academics. He demonstrates how to use play to find a concerted way to share the story of the company, organization, and/or university. Read more about this work at www.permission2play.com

Today you can find him teaching, among other courses, Applied Storytelling and Uncovering Fairytales, Folktales, and Ghost stories as a full time Assistant Professor at Ohio Dominican University. He also serves as co-director for the Columbus Area Writing Project at Ohio State University.

Dr. Cordi believes that his real learning occurred at the lap of his mother and father who raised him on stories of West Virginia. He believes that storytelling can change how a person learns. For over twenty-seven years, he has been playing with stories and refining how this can be done. You can find him at www.kevincordi.com

"Together we make a difference with stories."

Bibliography

Abbott, L. *Mantle of the Expert-An Attempt at Understanding the Misunderstood.* http://www.mantleoftheexpert.com/wp-content/uploads/2008/03/Teaching-Drama-2008-ArticleMoE-1.pdf.

Adler, M. *Writers at Play: Making the Space for Adolescents to Balance Imagination and Craft.* Portsmouth: Heinemann, 2009.

Baum, L. F. *The Lost Princess of Oz.* Champaign: Project Gutenberg, 1990.

Besser, M., I. Roberts, and M. Walsh. *The Upright Citizens Brigade Comedy Improvisation Manual.* Comedy Council of Nicea: Chicago, IL, 2013.

Bodkin, Odds. Storyteller, educator, author, musician. Personal communication.

Bonczek, R. B. and D. Storck, *Ensemble Theatre Making: A Practical Guide.* London: Routledge, 2013.

Booth, D. "Entering the Story Cave." *National Association for Drama in Education Journal* Vol. 18, No. 2 (1994): 37-45.

Booth, D. *Story Drama: Reading, Writing, and Roleplaying Across the Curriculum.* Markham, Ontario: Pembroke Publishers, 1994.

Booth, D. *Story Drama: Creating Stories through Role Playing, Improvising, and Reading Aloud.* Markham, Ontario: Pembroke Publishers, 2005.

Brooks, Simon. Personal communication, December 20, 2013.

Bruner, J. *Acts of Meaning.* Cambridge: Harvard University Press, 1990.

Bruner, J. "The Narrative Construction of Reality." *Critical Inquiry* Vol. 18, No. 1 (1991): 1-21.

Bruner, J. *The Culture of Education.* Harvard University Press, 1996.

Bruner, J. "The Narrative Construction of Reality." *Narrative Intelligence.* Edited by M. Mateas and Sengers. Amsterdam: John Benjamins Publishing Company, 2003.

Chambers, Aidan. *Tell Me: Children, reading and talking* Portland, ME: Stenhouse Publishers, 1996.

Clandinin, D.J. and F.M. Connelly. *Narrative Inquiry: Experience and Story in Qualitative Research*. San Francisco: Jossey-Bass, 2000.

Collins, R. and P.J. Cooper. *The Power of Story: Teaching Through Storytelling*. Scottsdale: Gorsuch Scarisbrick, 1997.

Cordi, K., "Teaching from Inquiry," *Content Area Reading, Writing, and Storytelling*. Westport: Libraries Unlimited, 2009.

Cordi, K. "Four Sites Profile: Using Drama in the Language Arts Classroom," *Ohio Journal of English Language Arts* Vol. 51, No. 2 (2011).

Cordi, K. and J. Carr. "Permission 2 Play: Using Ensemble Storytelling to Improve Writing: a Dialogue," *Ohio Journal of English Language Arts* Vol. 51, No. 2 (2011).

Cordi. K. "Digital Learning: Education 2.0: Misconceptions About Electronic Learning," *Ohio Resource Council Online*. Columbus, Ohio, 2012.

Cordi, K. "Using Drama to Create Fictional Worlds," *California English*, Vol 18, No.2 (2012).

Cordi, K. and K. Masturzo. "Reclaiming Cyberspace for Students: Using Literature and Digital Storytelling to Create a Safe Place to Address Bullying," *Voices from the Middle, a journal of the National Teachers of English*. San Diego, California, 2013.

Davis, D. *Telling Your Own Stories*. Little Rock: August House Publishers, 1993.

Davis, D. *Writing as a Second Language: From Experience to Story to Prose*. Little Rock: August House Publishers, 2000.

Davis, D. *What's Your Story?* Timpanogos Storytelling Institute, Orem, UT, 2012. DVD.

Dramaresource.com. *Hot-Seating*. http://dramaresource.com/strategies/hot-seating 2014

Dramaresource.com. *Tableaux*. http://www.dramaresource.com/strategies/tableaux 2014.

Dramaresource.com. *Thought Tracking*. http://www.dramaresource.com/strategies/thought-tracking 2014.

Duhigg, C. *The Power of Habit: Why We Do What We Do in Life and Business*. New York: Random House, 2012.

Dunne, W. T*he Dramatic Writer's Companion: Tools to Develop Characters, Cause Scenes, and Build Stories*. Chicago: The University of Chicago Press, 2009.

Ellis, Elizabeth. *From Plot to Narrative: A Step-by-Step Process of Story Creation and Enhancement*. Little Rock: Parkhurst Brothers, 2012.

Ellis, Elizabeth. *Every Day A Holiday: A Storyteller's Memoir*. Marion, MI: Parkhurst Brothers, 2014.

Edmiston, B. *Expert Positioning/Frame/Roles*. http://www.mantleoftheexpert.com/studying/articles/BE%20-%20Expert%20Positioning%20Frame%20Roles.pdf

Edmiston, B. *Forming Ethical Identities in Early Childhood Play*. London: Routledge, 2007.

Edmiston, B. Professor of Drama in Education, Ohio State University. Personal communication. 2009.

Edmiston, B. *What's My Position? Role, Frame, and Positioning When Using Process Drama*. http://www.mantleoftheexpert.com/wp-content/uploads/2012/04/Whats-my-position.pdf

Edmiston, B. *Transforming Teaching and Learning through Active Dramatic Approaches: Engaging Students Across the Curriculum*. London: Routledge, 2013.

Everman, Flavia. Storyteller. Personal communication. 2011.

Felice, C. *Weasel*. New York: Avon Books, Inc. 1991.

Gillard. Marni. "What I Believe, Do, or Know about Story Coaching." http://youthstorytelling.com/toolbox/ThoughtsonCoaching2.pdf.

Gillard, Marni. *Storyteller, Storyteacher: Discovering the Power of Storytelling for Teaching and Living*. York: Stenhouse Publishers, 1996.

Goldberg, N. *Writing Down the Bones: Freeing the Writer Within*. Boston: Shambhala, 1986.

Gottschall, J. *The Storytelling Animal: How Stories Make Us Human*. New York: Houghton Mifflin Harcourt, 2012.

Greenless, Rosy. Victoria and Albert Museum. *What is Craft?* http://www.vam.ac.uk/content/articles/w/what-is-craft/.

Hagen, U. and H. Frankel. *Respect for Acting*. New York: Macmillan, 1973.

Hagen, U., Du, K. Ludwig, *Uta Hagen's Acting Class* HB Studio, Applause Theatre & Cinema Books & Hal Leonard Publishing Corporation. New York: Applause Theatre & Cinema Books, 2002. DVD

Hanson, Lance. Storyteller. Personal communication.

Haven, K. "Story Smarts". http://www.kendallhaven.com/events.html

Haven, K. *Story Proof: The Science Behind the Startling Power of Story*. Westport: Libraries Unlimited, 2007.

Heathcote, D. Edited by L. Johnson, and C. O'Neill. Dorothy Heathcote: *Collected Writing on Education and Drama*. London: Hutchinson, 1984.

Heathcote, D. and G.M. Bolton. *Drama for Learning: Dorothy Heathcote's Mantle of the Expert Approach to Education*. Portsmouth, NH: Heinemann Press, 1995.

Hilbert, Vi. Teacher, storyteller, publisher, and public speaker. Personal Communication

Hillenburg, Kris. Audio podcast. "Hear Women Tell." http://www.herewomentell. com/archives/archives.html 2012.

Holland, R.W. *Deeper Writing: Quick Writes and Mentor Texts to Illuminate New Possibilities*. Thousand Oaks, CA: Corwin Press, 2013.

James, William *Talks to Teachers*. New York: Henry Holt and Company. 1925 The Gutenberg Project. http://www.gutenberg.org/files/16287/16287-h /16287-h.htm

Jeffers, S. *Feel the Fear and Do It Anyway*. New York: Random House, 1987.

Koste, V. Glasgow. *Dramatic Play in Childhood: Rehearsal for Life*. Portsmouth, Heinemann, 1995.

Larkin, Chuck. Bluegrass storyteller. Personal Communication.

Lave, J. and E. Wenger. *Situated Learning: Legitimate Peripheral Participation*. Cambridge: Cambridge University Press, 1991.

L'Engle, M. *Walking on Water: Reflections on Faith & Art*. Wheaton: H. Shaw, 1980.

Lipman, D. *The Storytelling Coach: How to Listen, Praise, and Bring Out People's Best*. Little Rock: August House, 1995.

Lipman, D. *Improving Your Storytelling: Beyond the Basics for All Who Tell Stories in Work or Play*. Little Rock: August House, 1999.

Martin, Rafe. Storyteller. Personal communication.

Maugham, W. Somerset, *Great Novelists and Their Novels*. J. C. Winston and Co., 1948.

Mendoza, Pat. Storyteller. Personal communication.

Milne, A. A. and E. H. Shepard. *The House at Pooh Corner*. New York: Dutton, 1961.

National Council of Teachers of English (NCTE). *Guideline on Teaching Storytelling*. http://www.ncte.org/positions/statements/teachingstorytelling 1992.

Neelands, J. *Making Sense of Drama, a Guide to Classroom Practice*. Portsmouth, Heinemann, 1984.

Neelands, J. and T. In Goode. *Structuring Drama Work: A Handbook of Available Forms in Theatre and Drama*. Cambridge: Cambridge University Press, 1991.

O'Callahan, Jay. Storyteller. Personal communication.

Ochs, E. and I. Capps. *Living Narrative: Creating Lives in Everyday Storytelling*. Cambridge: Harvard University Press, 2001.

O'Neill, C. *Drama worlds: a framework for process drama*. Portsmouth: Heinemann Press, 1995.

O'Neill, Cecily and Alan Lambert. *Drama Structures: A Practical Handbook for Teachers*. Portsmouth: Heinemann Press, 1982.

Peck, Richard. Author. Personal communication.

Plath, Sylvia. Editor K.V. Kukil. *The Unabridged Journals of Sylvia Plath*. New York: Anchor, 2000.

Radosavljević, D. *The Contemporary Ensemble: Interviews with Theatre-Makers*. London: Routledge, 2013.

Rogers, T., & C. O'Neill. Creating multiple worlds: Drama, language, and literary response. In G.E. Newell & R. R. Durst (Eds.), *Exploring Texts* (p 69-89), Norwood, MA: Christopher-Gordon, 1993

Sawyer, R. *The Way of the Storyteller*. New York: Viking Press, 1942.

Sagan, C. *Cosmos*. New York: Random House, 1980.

Schneider, Pat. *Writing Alone and with Others*. New York: Oxford University Press, 2003.

Schneider, Jenifer Jasinksi and Sylvia Jackson. "Process Drama: Special Space and Place for Writing," *The Reading Teacher*. V54, No.1: 38-51 (2000)

Sima, J. and K. Cordi. *Raising Voices: Creating Youth Storytelling Groups and Troupes*. Westport: Libraries Unlimited, 2003.

Simmons, A. *Whoever Tells the Best Story Wins: How to Use Your Own Stories to Communicate with Power and Impact.* New York: Amacon, 2007.

Spolin, V. *Improvisation for the Theater: A Handbook of Teaching and Directing Techniques.* Evanston: Northwestern University Press, 1963.

Spolin, V. *Improvisation for the Theater: A Handbook of Teaching and Directing Techniques.* Evanston: Northwestern University Press, 1983.

Spolin, V. *Theater Games for the Classroom: A Teacher's Handbook.* Evanston: Northwestern University Press, 1986.

Stone, R. *The Healing Art of Storytelling: A Sacred Journey of Personal Discovery.* New York: Hyperion, 1996.

Tolkien, J.R.R. *The Annotated Hobbit: The Hobbit, or, There and Back Again.* Boston: Houghton Mifflin Co., 1988.

Torrence, Jackie. Storyteller. Personal communication.

Vygotsky, L. (1978). "Problems of Method." *In Mind in Society.* Translated by M. Cole. Cambridge, MA: Harvard University Press, 1978.

Vonnegut, Kurt. "The Art of Fiction No. 64," *Paris Review.* http://www. theparisreview.org/interviews/3605/the-art-of-fiction-no-64-kurt-vonnegut

Wagner, J. Dorothy Heathcote: *Drama as a Learning Medium.* Washington: National Education Association, 1976.

Walsh, M., I. Roberts, M. Besser. *Upright Citizens Brigade Comedy Improvisation Manual.* New York: Comedy Council of Nicea, 2013.

Watterson, Bill. "Some thoughts on the real world by one who glimpsed it and fled". Commencement Address. http://web.mit.edu/jmorzins/www/C-H-speech. html

Welty, E. *One Writer's Beginnings.* Cambridge: Harvard University Press, 1984.

Wenger, E. *Communities of practice, a brief introduction.* http://wenger-trayner.com/ theory/

Wenger, E. *Communities of Practice: Learning, Meaning, and Identity.* New York: Cambridge University Press, 2000.

Yashinsky, Dan. Canadian storyteller.

L‌   ‌es at
www.parkhurstbrothers.com